Presenting and Training
with Magic!

Presenting and Training with Magic!

53 Simple Tricks You Can Use to
Energize Any Audience

Ed Rose

McGraw-Hill

New York   San Francisco   Washington, D.C.   Auckland   Bogotá
Caracas   Lisbon   London   Madrid   Mexico City   Milan
Montreal   New Delhi   San Juan   Singapore
Sydney   Tokyo   Toronto

Library of Congress Cataloging-in-Publication Data

Rose, Ed (Edwin)
    Presenting and training with magic! : 50 simple tricks you can
use to energize any audience / Ed Rose.
        p.   cm.
    ISBN 0-07-054041-1 (hc).—ISBN 0-07-054040-3 (pbk.)
    1. Tricks. 2. Conjuring. I. Title.
GV1547.R678   1997
793.8—dc21   97-41426
                                          CIP

1 2 3 4 5 6 7 8 9 0 EDW/EDW 9 0 0 9 8 7 6

ISBN 0-07-054040-3 (pbk.)
ISBN 0-07-054041-1 (cloth)

*The sponsoring editor for this book was Richard Narramore, the editing
supervisor was Fred Dahl, and the production supervisor was Tina
Cameron. It was set in New Century Schoolbook by Inkwell Publishing
Services.*

Printed and bound by Edwards Brothers, Inc.

This book is dedicated to my grandchildren—Justin, Jordan, Micah, and Taylor—
a legacy continuing the appreciation of magic in our family
and a lifelong desire for learning.
Be the best you can be!

Contents

Preface *xi*

Acknowledgments *xiii*

Seven Magic Principles for Presenters and Trainers *1*
Never let magic become more important than the message.

Magician's Aptitude Test *5*
Do you have what it takes to be a magician? The ultimate test of your intellectual abilities.

1. **Easy As 1–2–3** *15*
Mysteriously predict the numbers to be chosen by volunteers. An icebreaker or a metaphor for planning.

2. **I'm All Tied Up in This Argument** *19*
Demonstrate the importance of teamwork and creative problem solving.

3. **Dice Magic** *23*
See what others cannot see (the bottoms of dice)! Begin a discussion about perspectives, insight, and foresight. For small groups.

4. **1089** *25*
You can get the answer you want by asking the right question.

5. **True or False** *29*
A volunteer can lie, but your cards always tell the truth.

6. **Let's Meet Your Family** *31*
Tell the number of siblings and grandparents you have from a seemingly unrelated number. A metaphor for intelligent customer service.

7. **Magician Force** *35*
What seems like a free choice is actually forced by the magician. Use to emphasize a keyword.

8. **I Know What You're Thinking** *37*
That's how you stay a step ahead of the competition.

9. **The Power of the Mind** *41*
The mind can do magic on the body.

10. The Power of Teamwork   *43*
Show the power of teamwork!

11. Gray Elephant in Denmark   *47*
Demonstrate the power of asking good questions. Good for teaching facilitation skills.

12. The Structure of Teamwork   *49*
A hands-on puzzle for teams: Build a castle out of glasses and matches.

13. Let's Do the Twist   *51*
The power of visualization will twist you around.

14. Jenny's Mother Had Three Children   *53*
Demonstrate the importance of listening.

15. Wheel of Symbols   *55*
Symbolize expertise; predict a volunteer's secretly chosen position in a wheel of symbols.

16. The Age Teller   *59*
Guess the age of a volunteer. Stimulate a discussion on the importance of good systems.

17. Roman Finger Test   *63*
A humorous way to end a class. Can be used with any subject matter.

18. Restate the Problem (Balancing Glass)   *65*
Sometimes restating a problem can help solve it.

19. The Triple Backup   *69*
When you cover all the bases, the outcome is magic. Relates to good planning.

20. Needle through a Balloon   *71*
Put a large needle through a balloon without popping it. Discuss how to deal with change.

21. A Knotty Challenge   *73*
Only a fresh approach will get you out of a knot. A great example of out-of-the-box thinking.

22. Vanishing Napkin   *77*
Make a napkin disappear. If you don't pay close attention to things, things will go right over your head!

23. The Magic T   *81*
Solving problems sometimes requires us to look at problems from different angles.

24. What Is Synergy?   *85*
Three ropes of different lengths become equal in length when held together.

25. What's Your Name?   *91*
Names reveal a secretly chosen card.

26. Mind Reading Made Simple   *93*
Identify cards taken by volunteers by reading their minds.

27. The Power of the Living   *97*
Tell whether relatives are alive or dead by reading their names.

28. Torn and Restored Napkin   *99*
Inspiring illusion that says, Never give up!

29. Please Don't Make George Washington Cry   *103*
Harsh words make tears flow from a quarter. Harsh words can damage people's self-esteem.

30. Tear and Tear Alike   *105*
A simple puzzle requiring out-of-the-box thinking and an out-of-the-mouth solution. Stimulates creativity.

31. Pick Three   *109*
The top cards of randomly created stacks match the three cards you chose. Establish a good rapport with small groups.

32. The Teddy Bear Story   *113*
A delightful story about a teddy bear entertains and inspires the audience. Establish a warm rapport with the audience.

33. One-Dollar Trick   *117*
Transform two one-dollar bills into one two-dollar bill. Capture the attention of a small group.

34. The Incredible Card Reader   *123*
Read cards while they're inside a case. A hilarious trick with a ridiculously simple secret.

35. Return on Investment (ROI)   *125*
A $1 investment is magically transformed into a $100 return. Visualize ROI prior to financial training.

36. One-Liners and Anecdotes   *127*
Build a repertoire of one-liners and anecdotes to inject humor into your presentations.

37. Point to a Topic   *131*
A randomly selected card has today's presentation topic written on it.

38. The Easiest Mind-Reading Trick in the World   *133*
Correcly guess a volunteer's name. Works mainly with large audiences.

39. Money to Burn   *135*
After a dollar bill is burned, an indentical bill is produced. Was the bill burned or not?

40. That's Right   *137*
What starts out like a magic trick ends as a goofy joke.

41. Subliminal Suggestions   *139*
Influence a volunteer with subliminal suggestions. Doesn't always work but it's a surefire icebreaker.

42. Stuck on 13   *141*
Poor communication can make good organization ineffective.

Super Attention-Grabbing Tricks (Some Props Required)
Tricks 43–53 require you to buy inexpensive supporting gimmicks from a local or direct mail magic store (phone numbers provided). You will get a lot of bang for your buck!

43. The Magic Coloring Book   *145*
Magic crayons magically add color to a coloring book. Encourage the audience to "add color" to your workshop.

44. Levels of Trust   *147*
Do people really believe that you made water disappear? Demonstrate the different levels of trust in a relationship.

45. Harnessing Team Energy   *151*
The collective energy of the audience makes fire shoot from your hand.

46. The Impossible Is Possible   *155*
A bracelet passes right through a string. The impossible is possible.

47. Color-Changing Scarf   *157*
A scarf changes color as it passes between your hands. Symbolizes personal or organizational change.

48. It's the Last Key That Opens the Door   *159*
Illustrate that the key to success is perseverance.

49. Magic Keyword Speller   *161*
Randomly selected letters spell the keyword. Draw attention to a keyword.

50. Invisible Cards   *165*
Predict the card chosen out of an invisible deck of cards. Begin a discussion about imagination and perception.

51. A Hot Topic *169*
A book on a hot topic bursts into flames. The ulimate attention-grabber.

52. Floating Dollar Bill *171*
Float a dollar bill. Talk about money or positive thinking.

53. Fire to Rose *173*
A burning flame changes to a rose. Do a "visual check" on the audience.

Closing Comments *177*
A philosophical look at what makes a successful presenter.

Bibliography and Resources *179*

Preface

Magic is any mysterious, seemingly inexplicable,
or extraordinary power or influence.
—*According to Mr. Webster*

From early childhood, magic tricks captivated my interest, but I thought magic was too time-consuming and difficult to learn. I was also somewhat stage-shy and afraid to perform in front of others. Later in life, however, a career shift from production manager to trainer forced me onto the stage. Then I needed all the help I could get to grab the attention of the audience. I turned to magic.

After attending a special session on "Magic in Training" at a national conference of the American Society for Training and Development, I was inspired to attempt using magic in my training classes. I started small, with a basic card trick, and was amazed at the response from the participants. I slowly built my repertoire by adding a few tricks each week, and worked hard at relating them to the subject matter of my training classes. Before long, I was using magic in all my presentations. I learned that magic helped me to quickly establish a good rapport with the audience, making them more receptive to my message.

The purpose of this book is to help presenters make their presentations more entertaining and memorable by using magic tricks. The tricks I describe are elementary in technique but powerful in effect when performed with good *patter. Patter* is the term magicians use to describe the monologue delivered during the presentation of a trick. The patter is the most important part of the magician's performance because it creates suspense; it sets up the "a-ha" experience for the audience. For a presenter or trainer, the patter must do more than that. It must also make the trick relevant to the presentation.

This is one book you won't put on the shelf and forget. I describe 53 simple magic tricks and some possible uses, but I hope you will be inspired to modify the tricks to suit your own presentation topics. The introductory section, Seven Magic Principles for Presenters, should guide you in that effort. The Magic Principles encourage you to create opportunities for magic where you saw none before; they admonish you to make your magic elegant by keeping things simple and practicing your tricks. I wanted this book to be user-friendly. Each trick is self-contained, so the tricks can be studied in any order. I hope magic does for your presentations what it has done for mine all over the United States and Europe.

Some may say that this book should not have been written because it gives away magicians' secrets. While it does give away some basic magic tricks, it gives away no more than you would learn at a magic shop. This book will not make you a professional magician. Performing magic is an art; it's not learned by reading one book. If you would like to become a better magician, I urge you to join a local magic club or the International Brotherhood of Magicians.

Ed Rose

Acknowledgments

I'd like to thank two magicians who have influenced my work greatly:

John Anderson

Greg Phillips

I'd like to thank famous magicians who have contributed to my knowledge through their workshops and videos:

Aldo Colombini

Michael Ammar

Harry Anderson

Dai Vernon

Larry Becker

David Copperfield

Tony Hurley, from the Republic of Ireland

Tony Assini

Harry Allen

This project would have been impossible without the help of two very talented people:

Steve Buckley

Linda Woodall

Special thanks to those who gave me feedback on the magic tricks:

John Burchinal

Rick Manion

Wendy Jeffries

Irene Jones

Debbie Pierson

Steve Rose

Linda Becker

John Tankersley

Kurt Hoffman

Jennifer Odom

Al Genchi

Andrew Berman

Debra Seiloff

Eddie Rose

Denise King-Colon

Bonnie Clatterbough

Mike Yaffe

Scott Rose

Don Clatterbough

Photographs by:

Bob Goldberg

My deepest appreciation to my good friends and mentors:

Ray Odom

Dr. Louis Martin-Vega

And especially to my wife, Cheryl Ann. Thanks for being my audience.

The difference between a successful person and others is not a lack of strength, not a lack of knowledge, but rather a lack of will.

—Vince Lombardi

Seven Magic Principles for Presenters and Trainers

The Power of Magic

Today, a few closely guarded secrets of the world of magic are being successfully used in the corporate world to promote products, enhance workshops, and energize presentations. This book provides you with some of those secrets, modified for use in presentations, workshops, and seminars.

Think of the magic tricks described here as communication tools. These tools have been field-tested and are appropriate for absolute beginners. Tricks do not require sleight of hand. In fact, the secrets to most of the tricks are laws of mathematics and physics. The tricks are explained using easy-to-follow, step-by-step instructions. With these instructions, the tricks become nearly self-working. Your job is to create good "patter." Patter is the monologue you deliver during the trick to distract the audience from the secret of the trick, while entertaining them and relating the trick to your presentation. To help you create your patter, I provide you with sample patter for each trick.

Confidence and familiarity with your trick and your patter are the keys to using magic successfully in presentations. The following seven principles will help build your confidence.

1. Exude Personal Energy.

Before you step in front of an audience, do a quick check on your personal energy level. This is especially important when using magic tricks in your presentation. Kierkegaard said, "No learning can take place without emotion of some kind." Your patter consists of your demeanor, attitude, and gestures as much as the words you speak. You want to connect with your audience emotionally as well as rationally. We all have the potential for this ability—you don't have to be an Anthony Robbins or Tom Peters—let your confidence, humor, and warmth come out!

Once in front of an audience, be aware of your body movements and posture. Relax and be comfortable. This will make the audience relaxed and comfortable. Maintain good eye contact with the audience. Let a genuine, broad smile come through any nervousness you may feel. An important storytelling technique is to exaggerate your hand and body movements. Proper emphasis on tone and inflection of words is essential.

Performing a magic trick in a presentation is an art. It is anchored by your unique personality, amplified by technique, and honed through practice, but it is your personal energy that will breathe life into your performance. If you are not excited about your performance, who else will be?

end point. Keep in mind that good patter, not the mechanics of the trick, is the foundation of a magic trick.

If you should stumble a little in your presentation, don't worry. You are the only one who knows the whole trick and the patter. The audience is unlikely to catch small errors if you remain confident. Besides, magic is a tool to enhance your presentation; it is not the focal point of your presentation. A magic trick imperfectly performed can be repaired with smooth patter so that it has the same attention-grabbing effect on your presentation. A professional comedian once told me that the key to telling a joke well is knowing the punch line and not fumbling through it. Good presenters know the goals of their presentations. No matter how they change the middle of the story, they still have a strong and impressive finish.

2. Develop Patter That Fits.

The ultimate secret to a magician's success is not the mechanics of the trick; it's the presentation of the trick, or *patter,* as magicians refer to it. The simplest trick can be made to look like the world's greatest miracle, *if* the patter is good. The reverse is also true: The most ingenious magic trick can be a total flop if the patter is weak.

Each magic trick in this book includes sample patter. The patter I provide has worked for me in my presentations. The words may not always work for your presentation. If the sample patter doesn't seem right for you, adjust it to fit your personality and your presentation. The sample patter should be used as a starting point for your innovation, not the

3. Be Yourself.

Always be yourself, but be your best self. Push away the stage fright and self-consciousness that prevent your personality from shining through. Dramatic gestures, exaggerated facial expressions, and sound effects add life to a story. The more animated your patter, the more effective the magic.

On the other hand, don't try to be someone you're not. Don't contort your personality to fit those of other presenters and magicians; develop your own style. It's fine to adopt tricks and ideas from books and other magicians, but make sure they are adapted to fit your personality. If the audience expected to see David Copperfield, the ticket price would have been higher.

4. Remember the Golden Rule of Magic.

The Three Golden Rules of Magic are:

1. Practice
2. Practice
3. Practice

Practice in front of people who will give you specific feedback—people who will tell you what you *need* to hear rather than what you *want* to hear (don't we all need people like this for life in general?). Test all aspects of your trick, including patter. You should do a "live run" of the trick and the transition into or from the presentation. Your trick should add to your presentation, not distract from it. Be sure to ask your practice audience to evaluate this aspect.

Practice before each performance. It is tempting to feel that because you remember the order of events, no practice is needed. Remembering the mechanics of a trick isn't the same as perfecting the trick. I learned this lesson the hard way. Once I dusted off a trick I used to perform, and without practicing it again I used it in a workshop, only to have it fail. That was embarrassing, but it was a valuable lesson. Now I practice each trick before every presentation regardless of how well I think I know it. Practicing before a performance is especially important in making sure that your patter fits well with the particular presentation you are going to give.

5. Never Reveal the Secret of Your Trick.

Although everyone wants to believe in magic, most people still want to know the secret to a magic trick. But if you reveal the secret, you'll ruin the audience's sense of wonder and, in the end, they'll be disappointed at knowing the secret rather than amazed. A magician once told me that magic is like Christmas. When we see all those gifts under the Christmas tree we want to peek inside the gift wrap and find out what's in them. If we do peek, the mystery and excitement we felt vanishes. So it is with magic; once the secret is out, the magic is gone.

Magicians only share their secrets with other magicians. The sharing is a part of their fellowship. They share and improve their secret methods in order to bring more joy to more people. Carelessly spilling the secrets will destroy the very effect this book was designed to help you create—which is to spark the audience's imagination with a flash of the mystical.

An important corollary to this rule is, "Never do the same trick twice for the same audience." When someone says, "Do that again," what the person really wants is to see your secret. You should reply with something like, "That's against the magic code." If someone asks you how you did a trick, you should reply, "Very well, thank you!"

6. Customize Your Magic.

Customizing magic tricks to fit your presentation is an acquired skill. It should improve with practice. Let your imagination and intuition guide you. Given a particular presentation, you may learn a whole new magic trick that fits in. Maybe all that is needed is to modify a known magic trick a little to fit the presentation, or vice versa. Or maybe you just need to see an old trick under a new light—to innovate! To clarify what I mean by "innovate" let me tell a short story about invention and innovation.

At the turn of the century, there was a famous German chemist named Adolf von Baeyer. In 1905 he won the Nobel Prize in chemistry. One morning, Baeyer came into his laboratory and found that his assistants had built an ingenious mixing device operated by water turbines. The professor was fascinated with the complex machine, and he summoned his wife to show her the marvelous invention. Frau Baeyer stared at the apparatus silently for a minute. Then she exclaimed, "What a lovely idea for making mayonnaise!"

There is an important difference between the good professor's students and his wife. The students invented. Frau Baeyer *innovated*. You can be an innovator by giving new life to the magic tricks in this book. You might surprise yourself with your ability to innovate. Innovators bring magic to life.

7. Simple Is Best.

Your magic tricks should be simple. Obeying the KISS principle ("Keep It Simple, Silly") has many benefits. Simple tricks are easier to learn. Simple tricks are easier to adapt. Simplicity of a trick isn't related to its effectiveness; good patter can make the simplest trick seem like a miracle. Besides, your presentation should be the focus, not the magic trick. Don't get carried away by your magic.

How to Use This Book

The Table of Contents lists many attention-grabbing tricks and how they

might be used, but these recommendations are not the final word. Once you understand the Seven Magic Principles for Presenters and Trainers, and have practiced some of the tricks, you should be ready to customize them to fit your specific needs and audiences.

First, to learn a new trick, read the entire description to get the big picture of the trick. Next, study *The Trick, Step by Step* and practice the mechanics of the trick until you are thoroughly comfortable. Third, invent a good patter or modify the given *Sample Patter* and practice speaking it. Finally, combine the mechanics of the trick with the patter, and practice, practice, practice! Be sure to practice in front of a small test audience (friends or associates) and invite their critique.

The magic tricks in this book have helped my presentations enormously and I'm convinced they will do the same for you. Feel free to e-mail me if you have any problems understanding a trick (ER1495@AOL.COM). You can also visit my Internet homepage at:

http://www.geocities.com/Athens/ 2326.

Good luck on your upcoming presentation!

Ed Rose

Magician's Aptitude Test

Do YOU have what it takes?

> **Honor Code:** *Please don't get help from others or jump ahead to the answers.*

If you can pass this test, you can perform the tricks and attention-grabbers in this book. Dr. Justin Micah-Rose worked for months matching technical competencies to each of these test questions. We feel extremely confident in the validity of this test, and hope that you find some value in it once you have completed it.

Good luck, and *let the force be with you*! Above all, ***don't panic***!!!

Find the Panda

There is a panda hiding in the back of this pickup truck. Can you find it?

YES _____   NO _____

Connect the Dots

1.

2.

Word Search

Find the word in the word list by looking across, down, and diagonally, and circle the word you find.

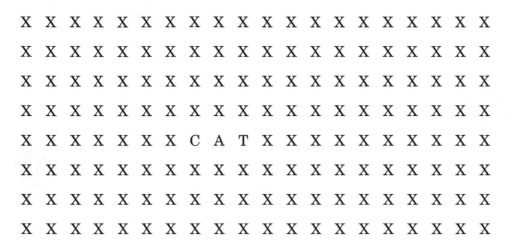

```
X  X  X  X  X  X  X  X  X  X  X  X  X  X  X  X  X  X
X  X  X  X  X  X  X  X  X  X  X  X  X  X  X  X  X  X
X  X  X  X  X  X  X  X  X  X  X  X  X  X  X  X  X  X
X  X  X  X  X  X  X  X  X  X  X  X  X  X  X  X  X  X
X  X  X  X  X  X  C  A  T  X  X  X  X  X  X  X  X  X
X  X  X  X  X  X  X  X  X  X  X  X  X  X  X  X  X  X
X  X  X  X  X  X  X  X  X  X  X  X  X  X  X  X  X  X
X  X  X  X  X  X  X  X  X  X  X  X  X  X  X  X  X  X
```

What Animal Is This?

Guess the animal in the incomplete drawing.

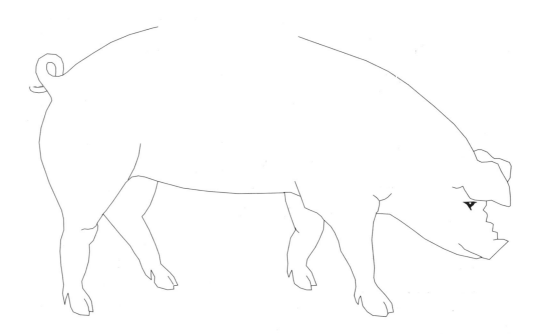

Write your answer here: _____

Then see if you can complete the drawing.

The Maze

Get through the maze!

START

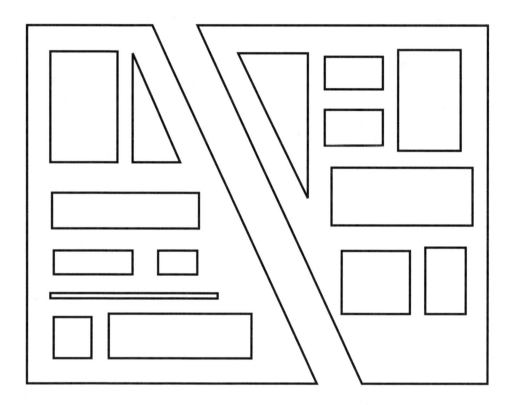

FINISH

Which Animal Is Different?

One of these pictures is different from the others. Can you find it?

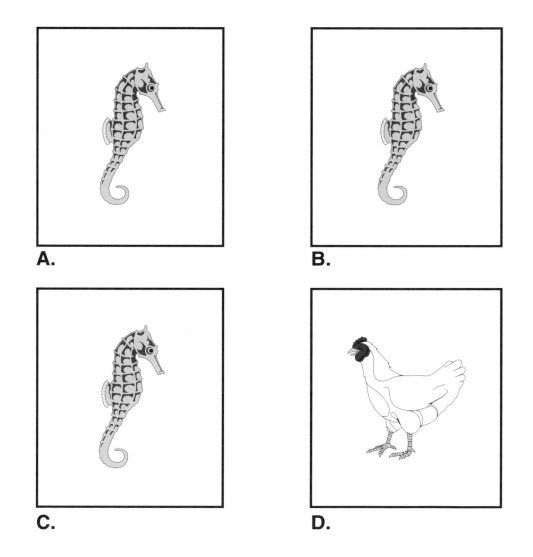

A.

B.

C.

D.

Write your answer here _____

Pick the Bigger One

Which is bigger?

A. Pineapple

B. Pea

Write your answer here _____

Score Yourself

Test Questions	Answer Key	Score
Find the Panda	Yes	+1
Connect the Dots	1 •——————• 2	+1
Word Search	Cat	+1
What Animal Is This?	Pig	+1
The Maze		+1
Which Animal Is Different?	D	+1
Pick the Bigger One	A	+1
Total Score (if you get them all correct)		7

Give yourself 1 point for each item answered correctly.

If you scored at least a 2 on the test, you should be capable of learning some basic magic tricks. But before we start, I want to borrow a powerful quote from Charles Swindoll about attitude and its importance. He said:

The longer I live, the more I realize the impact of attitude on life. Attitude, to me, is more important than the past, than education, than money, than circumstances, than failures, than successes, than what other people think or say or do. It is more important than appearance, giftedness or skill. It will make or break a company ... a church ... a home. The remarkable thing is we have a choice every day regarding the attitude we will embrace for that day. We cannot change our past ... we cannot change the fact that people will act in a certain way. We cannot change the inevitable. The only thing we can do is play on the one string we have, and that is our attitude ... I am convinced that life is 10% what happens to me and 90% how I react to it. And so it is with you ... we are in charge of our attitudes.

If you approach this book with the attitude that you are going to make things happen and learn something new, you will find this book very valuable. In addition to the magic tricks, it is full of humor and anecdotes that can help you grab people's attention. As a presenter, you always want to keep an upbeat, positive, and confident attitude. It will be this attitude, expressed in your presentation of both the tricks and your messages, that will ultimately be the key to your success. The goal is to come off as being sure of yourself, not condescending to your audience. Combine a good attitude, a good message, and enthusiasm—and the audience is yours!!

Background

This trick has a long history with a close friend of mine, a local magician named John Anderson. It's a great trick for beginners, no props are involved, and you *will* get looks of wonder from the audience, especially your volunteers.

The Magical Effect

You astonish the audience by predicting the numbers to be chosen by three volunteers.

Applying the Magic to Presenting and Training

Although the essence of this trick is very simple, the trick has wide applicability. With some practice, you should be able to apply the trick to any size group of volunteers. By inventing good patter (the story setting up the trick), you can make this trick relevant to many situations. Some ways I've used this trick are:

- as an icebreaker,
- as a metaphor for planning ahead,
- as a symbol of teamwork (when used with a partner).

Materials

- 1 thick marker
- 3 large sheets of paper
- Tape or tacks

Easy as 1-2-3

"Only those who have the patience to do simple things perfectly acquire the skill to do difficult things easily."

—*Unknown*

The Trick, Step by Step

Step 1:

Write the numbers 1, 2, and 5 on one sheet of paper without showing the audience, cover it with a second sheet, and post it in a visible place.

Step 2:

Select three volunteers and ask each to think of a number between 1 and 100. You will be asking them to do some simple math calculations, so make sure each has a pen or pencil and paper. Ask the volunteers to write their number down, but keep it to themselves.

Step 3:

Ask the volunteers to double their numbers.

Step 4:

Ask volunteer #1 to add 2 to the number.

Ask volunteer #2 to add 4 to the number.

Ask volunteer #3 to add 10 to the number.

Step 5:

Ask the volunteers to divide their numbers by 2.

Step 6:

Ask the volunteers to subtract the original numbers from the result in Step 5.

Step 7:

Ask the volunteers to write their numbers on a large piece of paper, and post it next to the covered piece of paper. Reveal the numbers you wrote.

If you do a little algebra, you can see that the key to the trick is the number you give the volunteers for addi-

tion (Step 4). The answers will be halves of these numbers.

Sample Patter

(Patter is the story a magician tells while performing a trick. Often the patter is more important than the trick itself.) I have used this trick for many different presentations, but one example is a workshop I deliver on manufacturing processes. I introduce the trick as follows:

"I was thinking about manufacturing [process] and the people working with manufacturing [process], and in the [process] I thought of three numbers." Patter should tell your story—it should make a point—and distract the audience from the mechanics of the trick. I repeat the word [process] to distract the audience from the basic math. After all, it is the topic of the workshop! "I wrote the numbers on a piece of paper and posted the paper in front of you. Now I need three volunteers for this [process]." It's always a good idea to reward the volunteers with something—something as simple as applause is encouraging. Once they choose their numbers, I tell them we are going to "put you through a manufacturing process." When the trick ends and I have mysteriously predicted their numbers I say, "Now I am a gifted mind reader, but I chose not to use my powers just now. I put the volunteers through a carefully controlled process, and I got just the results I planned for, as predicted. That's what a good manufacturing process is all about."

Remember, the "patter" you use when you perform this trick will be different from the manufacturing-related patter I use here. This sample patter is intended to give you an example and get your creative storytelling juices flowing. This trick can be used in all kinds of training contexts, if you create the right patter to go with it.

Because the key to the trick is so simple, this trick can be played with the whole workshop if you develop a system to remember what number you gave to each person. This trick also plays well at dinner or lunch with friends or customers. Be sure to invent good patter—a tall tale to show off your psychic ability.

Note: The secret is the number you give should be even and your answer should be exactly half of it.

Debriefing

In the workshop scenario given above, after performing the trick I say, "We're here today to discuss process controls and how important they are to successfully manufacture a product. What kind of process did I use in predicting the numbers? Who or what controlled the process? How could you improve the process? Let's talk about your work process ...."

Background

This trick was shared with me by a teacher who used it in a very different way than I'm describing here. When she explained it to me, I knew immediately what I could use it for. I was like a kid at Christmastime! Just wait—when you get the magic bug, you'll have the same response. This one has a lot of possibilities for variation.

The Magical Effect

Two participants are tied together and asked to free themselves from each other. The task seems hopeless, but you open their eyes by showing them an ingenious solution.

Applying the Magic to Presenting and Training

This trick can be used as:

- an exercise in a conflict-resolution workshop or creative problem-solving class;

- an energizer for a planning session, illustrating the need for fresh approaches to an old problem;

- an example of the need for collaboration.

Consider having the two volunteers on stage so that everyone can easily observe them. Alternatively, you can have everyone tied together in pairs. Be sure to have enough rope. You may want to have an assistant to help with large groups so you can stay on stage.

I'm All Tied Up in This Argument

For every minute you're angry, you lose sixty seconds of happiness.

Materials

- 2 six-foot pieces of rope (thick rope is preferred)

The Trick, Step by Step

Step 1:

Take one piece of rope and tie it between the wrists of volunteer #1. Before you tie up volunteer #2, link the two ropes by putting one end under the other rope before tying it (Fig. 2-1). Ask the volunteers to untangle themselves.

Step 2:

After the volunteers have struggled unsuccessfully for a while, provide them with the solution. Have volunteer #1 put both arms out straight. Volunteer #2 should create a loop with his or her rope and pass it through the knotted loop around volunteer #1's wrist (Fig. 2-2). (The direction from which volunteer #2's loop enters

volunteer #1's knotted loop is important; please follow Fig. 2-2 carefully.) Volunteer #2 then passes the loop over volunteers #1's hand (Fig. 2-3), stretches his or her arms out as far as the rope will allow and steps back. Now they're free! (Fig. 2-4)

Sample Patter

As you are tying the two volunteers together (as described above), explain that the ropes symbolize a conflict these two are having. Invent and describe a conflict relevant to the theme of your presentation. Ask the volunteers to untangle themselves without cutting or untying the rope (that would be too easy). **Very few** participants will solve the problem in five minutes. After some discussion, present your solution, explaining that it requires a collaborative approach. "To resolve conflicts, it's much more effective to cooperate than to battle against one another." As an option, you may bring in a third volunteer as a mediator who can help them find a solution, or involve the entire audience, explaining, "The volunteers have tried to work on the problem alone. Can anyone suggest a better solution?" You can also use this trick to illustrate the need for people to look for new and creative approaches to old problems (paradigm shifts!).

Debriefing Questions

- How did you originally approach the problem?
- How did you find the solution?
- What helped you see the problem from a different angle?
- How do you approach conflicts in your work environment?

Figure 2-1

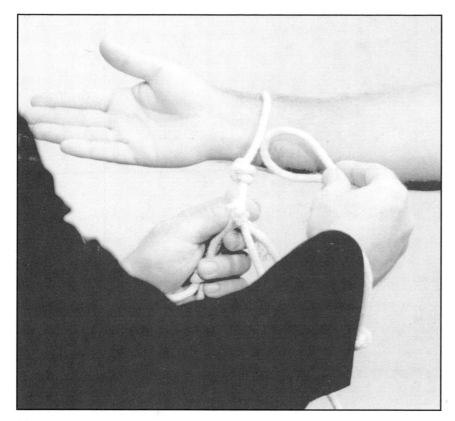

Figure 2-2

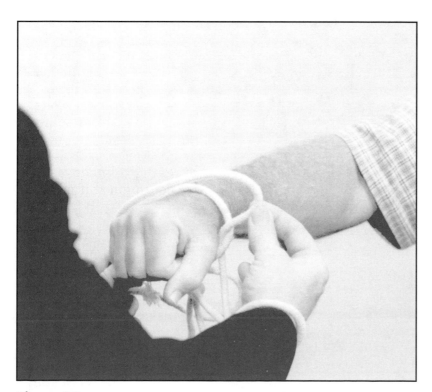

Figure 2-3

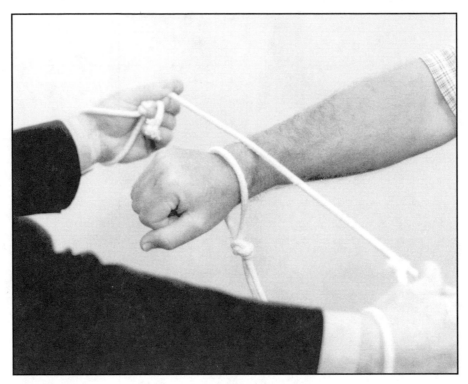

Figure 2-4

Background

An associate of mine, Steve Buckley, shared this trick with me. I've had some fun with this one. The KISS principle (see Magic Principle #7, page 4) is at work here.

The Magical Effect

A volunteer rolls three dice, and just by looking at the number's that come up you can tell the sum of the numbers on the *bottoms* of the dice.

Applying the Magic to Presenting and Training

Be especially creative with your patter for this trick. The better the theatrics, the more memorable this trick will be. This trick can lead into a variety of topics:

- the importance of seeing all angles of a problem,
- the importance of establishing a simple and effective system,
- the importance of insight.

Or you may use the trick to simply impress and amuse people.

Some people will know the secret of the trick because of their familiarity with dice. That's all right. This does not detract from its usefulness in launching a discussion. You can be assured, however, that 90 percent of your audience won't have a clue how it works.

Materials

- 3 dice
- A table

Trick #**3**

Dice Magic

A moment's insight is sometimes worth a lifetime's experience.

The Trick, Step by Step

Step 1:

Ask a volunteer to roll three dice on a table.

Step 2:

Silently add the numbers on the *top* of the dice. Twenty-one minus this sum is equal to the sum of the numbers on the bottoms of the dice.

Sample Patter

This trick works best for a small group. It's a good reason to take three dice with you to a personal meeting or a casual business lunch. I usually tell the following story tongue-in-cheek, combined with some theatrics. "A Zen master once said to his students, 'It takes the eye of faith to see the undeveloped butterfly in the caterpillar.' Well, as with the Zen master, I see beyond what others see. I see I have three dice in my right pocket." Taking out the dice and intently putting them into the hands of someone at the table, I declare, "I see one of you rolling these dice on the table." After someone has rolled the dice, I put on an anguished face and exclaim, "I can just barely see through the top of the dice down to the bottom of the dice. I think that the numbers on the bottom add up to eleven!" I ask someone in my audience to add up the total of the numbers on the bottom of the dice. When they confirm that I have guessed correctly I observe, "Ah, I see! I see that we are ready to take a five-minute coffee break."

Debriefing Questions

- What does what you see tell about what you don't see?

- Do you easily see all the angles to a problem?

- Is your work system simple and effective?

- Why is it important to be able to predict outcomes in a service or manufacturing environment?

- How can you relate this to your work environment?

Background

This trick has been around for a long time. I used this one even before I became interested in magic as a presentation tool. I'm including it because it has a great effect and it fits the "KISS" principle (see Magic Principle #7, page 4).

The Magical Effect

A volunteer selects a number, and you guess it by reading his or her thought waves.

Applying the Magic to Presenting and Training

- An icebreaker
- An example of a foolproof system
- Entertainment

Materials

- 2 large pieces of paper
- 1 pen
- 1 large object such as a briefcase (for conducting "thought waves" between you and the volunteer)

The Trick, Step by Step

Step 1:

Ask a volunteer to think of a three-digit number. It must consist of three different numbers.

Step 2:

Place an object between your face and the volunteer's and act as if you are reading the volunteer's mind. Explain that brain waves

---

| Trick #4 |

1089

Thinking is like living and dying ... each of us must do it for ourselves.

are passing between you and the volunteer, through the object. After you've "read" the volunteer's mind, write "1089" on a piece of paper without letting anyone see it, then cover it.

Step 3:

Ask the volunteer to write the number he or she picked on a piece of paper, and perform the following calculations:

- Reverse the order of the digits.
- Compare the two numbers on the page, and subtract the smaller from the larger.
- Add a zero to the front if the answer is a two-digit number.
- Take the resulting amount and reverse the order of the digits.
- Add this new number to the previous number.

Step 4:

Ask the volunteer if he or she freely chose the original number and told it to no one. Reveal the number you wrote. If the volunteer's math is done correctly, (watch to make sure it is) the result of the volunteer's calculations should always be 1089.

Note: When a number ending in a zero is reversed, the result should begin with a zero. For example, 270 becomes 072 when reversed. If the number remaining after subtraction is a two-digit number, add a leading zero to the number before continuing. Guide the volunteer through Step 3 again if you don't arrive at 1089.

Taking the audience's attention away from the mechanics of the trick is crucial to the success of the trick. How you present the trick will make it look either like a miracle or like just another math trick.

Sample Patter

"I'd like to try something I recently learned on a trip to a special place, though I'm not at liberty to share the location. It's really not important, anyway. At this place, a Zen master demonstrated how I could become one with a person by connecting our thought waves. This was a great experience and I was actually able to read other people's thought waves. The Zen master told me it was due to the positive energies in the group. However, I've never done this with nonbelievers. So, with your permission, before we start I'd like to practice for the first time in public." I've never had a group refuse, but you should be prepared for that to happen. If the audience refuses, choose a response you're comfortable with. For example, I'd say, "Okay, I'll do it anyway."

I select a volunteer and ask, "Select a three-digit number. The three digits in the number must be different, but don't tell me your number." A little acting helps here—remember the Seven Magic Principles. Pick up an object and have the volunteer hold one end while you hold the other. You can also hold the volunteer's hand or touch in some way, depending on the audience's view of political correctness. I say, "Concentrate on the three-digit number you thought of," and for about 15 seconds I give my best impression of a Zen master at work. While doing this, I may ask the group, "Do you know what I'm doing? This is what I learned from the Zen master, and I'm getting in contact with your thought waves. It will help if you all believe, promoting the positive energy in the room."

After I've "read" my volunteer's mind and guided him or her through converting the number, I ask, "Did you have a free choice in selecting your number? Did I have any influence on the number you selected?" I may ask several more questions like these. I try hard to take the audience's attention away from the math. Then I say, "Okay, let's see the results of my first public attempt at connecting on your thought waves. This could make my Zen master proud." Instead of announcing the number myself, I ask the volunteer to read it aloud. This emphasizes that he or she freely chose the number. If the volunteer

doesn't say 1089, I quickly respond, "Okay. Let's review your thought process," and look for mistakes in the math. Once I've located the error, I lead the volunteer through the steps again.

I end by saying, "Well, my Zen master would be proud of me, and this tells me we will have a good session today, because there are positive energies in the room. This couldn't have happened if there was a lot of negative energy in the room. It's going to be a great day!"

Background

This is an easy-to-learn, self-working card trick with mind-boggling results. No sleight of hand is necessary; all you do is ask a volunteer to count out cards according to a recipe and the result is magical.

The Magical Effect

A volunteer is asked to shuffle and select one of nine cards. The volunteer is then asked to count out the cards while spelling out the identity of the selected card. The volunteer is allowed to lie when spelling, but the truth comes out anyway: The selected card is found at the top of the stack.

Applying the Magic to Presenting and Training

Because the trick revolves around the idea of lying and telling the truth, it can be used to open any presentation related to ethics. It's relevant to teamwork too: I use the trick to argue that, no matter what, the truth comes out in the end. It's a good icebreaker for small groups.

Materials

- 1 deck of cards

The Trick, Step by Step

Step 1:

Ask a volunteer to shuffle a deck of cards and select nine cards, setting aside the remainder. Ask the volunteer to shuffle the nine cards and deal them into three stacks of three cards each.

Trick #5

True or False

The best way to command respect is to be worthy of it.

Step 2:

Ask the volunteer to pick one of the three stacks and memorize the bottom card of that stack. Ask the volunteer to put the selected stack on top of one of the two remaining stacks and then put the combined stack on top of the third stack.

Step 3:

Tell the volunteer that it's optional to lie or tell the truth about the identity of the memorized card. Ask the volunteer to hold the combined stack of nine cards and spell out the value of the memorized card, putting down a card (into a stack) face down for each letter. For example, three cards should be laid down for a card whose value is two (there are three letters in "two"). Use "eleven" for jacks, "twelve" for queens, "thirteen" for kings, and "fourteen" for aces. Ask the volunteer to put the remaining cards on top of the stack.

Step 4:

Ask the volunteer to pick up the stack of cards and spell "of," putting down a card (into a stack) for each letter. Ask the volunteer to put the remaining cards on top of the stack.

Step 5:

Reminding the volunteer of the option to lie or tell the truth about the identity of the memorized card, ask him or her to pick up the stack of cards and spell the suit of the memorized card, putting down a card (into a stack) for each letter. Ask the volunteer to put the remaining cards on top of the stack.

Step 6:

Ask the volunteer, "Did you tell the *truth* about the card, or was what

you said *false*?" If the volunteer answers "truth," ask him or her to spell "truth," putting down a card for each letter. If the volunteer answers "false," ask him or her to spell "false," putting down a card for each letter. Turn over the last card put down (the fifth one)—it should be the one that the volunteer memorized earlier. Ask the volunteer if this card is indeed the card that was memorized earlier.

Sample Patter

"Good morning. Before we start our session today, I would like to conduct a little exercise in personal ethics. Could I have a volunteer willing to demonstrate its effectiveness?" While the volunteer is shuffling the deck of cards, I ask the audience how they established their personal ethics and how they feel about telling lies. After a brief discussion with the audience, I have the volunteer deal out three stacks of three cards each and announce that the lie detector is ready to be tested.

Debriefing Questions

- How did you feel when you lied? How does it contrast with when you tell the truth?
- Did the presence of the group influence your decision to lie or tell the truth?
- Did our brief discussion about personal ethics influence your decision to lie or tell the truth?
- Are there legitimate reasons to lie in the workplace?
- What do you think about lying among team members?

Background

This trick has been around since at least the 1920s, but it plays very well with audiences. It's complex enough to confuse everyone except the real mathematicians in the audience.

The Magical Effect

You ask a volunteer to do some seemingly complex math, and based only on the result you can magically tell the number of living grandparents, brothers, and sisters the volunteer has.

Applying the Magic to Presenting and Training

Because you are able to magically interpret information given by a volunteer, this trick is a good metaphor for customer service. (Good customer service people should be able to know what customers' needs are even if they're not clearly articulated.) The trick also works as an ice-breaker to get people talking about their family or personal lives, or to introduce a problem-solving discussion. The trick can be used with many volunteers. Simply have all the volunteers go through the math together; you can then interpret the resulting numbers one at a time.

Materials

- 1 piece of paper and pen or pencil for each volunteer

(Although many volunteers will be able to do the math in their heads, some may feel more comfortable having a paper and pen.)

Trick	#6

Let's Meet Your Family

Too bad I didn't have all my troubles when I was twenty-one—that was when I knew everything!

—*Unknown*

The Trick, Step by Step

Step 1:

Ask the volunteers to take the number of brothers they have, double it, add 3 to the result, then multiply that number by 5.

Step 2:

Ask the volunteers to add the number of sisters they have to the result from the previous step, then multiply the result by 10.

Step 3:

Ask the volunteers to add the number of living grandparents they have to the result from the previous step, and subtract 150 from the result.

Step 4:

The first digit of the number is the number of brothers. The second digit is the number of sisters. The last digit is the number of living grandparents. For example, if the result is 213, there are two brothers, one sister, and three living grandparents.

You may want to use the worksheet provided.

Sample Patter

"I would like to demonstrate a system for discovering things about a customer by interpreting a few seemingly unrelated numbers. I will use a subject that we are all familiar with—family members. I'm going to ask you to do a little math." After I guide several volunteers through the math, I ask them, one person at a time, "What number did you come up with?" When they tell me the numbers, I ask the audience, "Does anybody know from this number the number of brothers, sisters, and living grandparents this person has? It would appear impossible, doesn't it? I believe that if we ask smart questions of our customers and interpret their answers intelligently, we can serve them better. Here's what I gathered by listening closely to the data my customers just gave me about their families ..." (then I "wow" the audience by announcing what I've deduced about the volunteers' families and have the volunteers confirm my deductions to the audience.)

_____ (# of brothers)

x   **2**

=   _____

+   **3**

=   _____

x   **5**

=   _____

+   _____ (# of sisters)

=   _____

x   **10**

=   _____

+   _____ (# of living grandparents)

=   _____

-    **150**

=   _____

Background

Magicians allow participants to choose cards freely 90 percent of the time. There are times, however, when what appears to be free choice is really "magician force." Magician force means that what seems like a free choice is actually forced by the magician. There are as many ways to force a card as there are grains of sand on a beach! I'm going to share with you a very basic force that most people won't catch on to.

The Magical Effect

Four cards are placed face down on a table. A volunteer is asked to make a series of card choices and you discard cards based on the cards they choose. You flip over the remaining card and the audience is amazed that the card has written on it a keyword relating to the presentation.

Applying the Magic to Presenting and Training

This trick can be used to start a session or end a session. It lets you reiterate a keyword in a fun manner. Because the secret of this trick is simple, it can be modified for numerous situations. This trick can be used with small or large groups, depending on the visuals you use and the way you set it up.

Materials

- 4 playing cards, with a keyword written on one of them

Trick #7
Magician Force

The best way to predict the future is to create it.
—*Stephen Covey*

The Trick, Step by Step

Step 1:

Lay four cards on a table, face down. Remember which one has the keyword written on it.

Step 2:

Ask a volunteer to point to two cards. If their choices include the card with the word written on it, then discard the other two cards. If their choices do not include the card with the word written on it, then discard the chosen cards.

Step 3:

Ask another volunteer to point to one of the two remaining cards. Discard the card without the word written on it. Reveal the card with the word written on it.

Discuss the topic of your presentation for a few minutes at every step to distract the participants from the "magician force" and integrate this trick into your presentation. Remember, as soon as you tell people you are going to do a magic trick, people will watch you very closely to try to catch you. If you remember the "stay one step ahead" principle, this will be another trick that will make you a legend in your own backyard! Be sure to consider Magic Principles #5, #6, and #7 when preparing for this trick. This trick can be used in many different ways with just a few simple modifications. Yes, I can hear you saying that this trick is too simple and that no one would possibly fall for it. Try it, and you'll be surprised!

Sample Patter

I may conclude a workshop on the theme of trust by saying this: "Well, that brings us to the close of this section. I need a volunteer to help me. Who would like to give me a hand with this?" I select a volunteer, then ask the audience some questions related to the workshop that can **and should** be answered with the word trust. After a few questions, I inquire whether the audience agrees that "Trust is the foundation of all relationships." Some don't agree and that's okay, because what happens next will change their minds. I ask the volunteer to point to two of the four cards. I show the cards to be discarded to the class. I never use the word "choose"; I prefer to use the word "point" instead. After discarding the two cards, I ask the volunteer to point to one of the two remaining cards. Then I say, "You had a free choice, and if trust is indeed the foundation of all human relationships, this card would confirm it." I then show the remaining card to the class, and, written on it, in big letters, is the word "Trust."

Background

I'd like to say "Thanks!" to a special friend of mine, a great magician in his own right, Greg Phillips. He was nice enough to share this trick with me. I used this trick in both the United States and Europe with great success. This is a surefire showstopper, and even if you are a beginning magician, some people will swear that you're the next David Copperfield!

The Magical Effect

Volunteers choose one of four symbols on a card without revealing their choice to you. Simply by having them point out the card with their chosen symbol, you guess which symbol they chose.

Applying the Magic to Presenting and Training

This trick illustrates that having a good system is like magic. It can open a discussion on customer service and competition. It may be used to open a sales call or as product promotion by using cards with product symbols on them.

Materials

- 4 symbol cards (Fig. 8-3)

The Trick, Step by Step

Step 1:

Select four volunteers who are sitting apart from each other, so that it is easy for you to remember their order.

Trick #**8**

I Know What You're Thinking

*The most important thing in communication is to hear what **isn't** being said.*
—Peter F. Drucker

Step 2:

Show the front of the first card to the first volunteer, and have him or her pick a symbol without revealing it. Do the same with the second card and the second volunteer, the third card and the third volunteer, and the fourth card and the fourth volunteer. (See Fig. 8-1)

Step 3:

Flip through the cards and show the first volunteer the backs of the cards (Fig. 8-2). Ask the volunteer to say "stop" when you come to the card with his or her chosen symbol. The symbol the volunteer chose is the third symbol on the current card.

Step 4:

Repeat Step 3 with each of the remaining volunteers. To find the chosen symbol, add 2 to the order of the volunteer. For example, the second volunteer's symbol is the fourth ($2 + 2 = 4$) symbol on the current card. The third volunteer's symbol is the fifth ($3 + 2 = 5$) symbol, which is actually the first symbol on the card (you "wrap around" to the first symbol when counting).

It is important that you do not confuse the fronts of the cards with the backs, and that you remember the order of the cards. Position the cut ends of the cards to your upper right to show the front of the cards (Fig. 8-1). Position the cut ends to your upper left to show the back of the cards (Fig. 8-2). Prepare the cards so that the cut edge of the first card has one small notch, the second card two, the third card three, and the fourth card four (Fig. 8-3). By noting the

number of small notches, you can keep the cards in order. Alternatively, you can memorize the order of the symbols: A circle is the first symbol on the first card; a plus-sign is the first symbol on the second card; three squiggly lines make up the first symbol on the third card; a square is the first symbol on the fourth card.

The less time you spend staring at and handling the cards, the more convincing the magic is. Remember Magic Principle #3 ("Practice, practice, practice!").

Sample Patter

"I would like to demonstrate how important it is to stay one step ahead of your competition. If you can do this you can almost read people's minds." After strategically selecting four volunteers, I often remind them, "Please don't forget your symbol; write it down if you want to." Most won't forget. After I correctly identify their chosen symbols, I declare, "This wasn't magic. I had a system that allowed me to stay one step ahead of you and it appeared that I was reading your minds. This is what we need to do when helping our customers."

Debriefing Questions

- How can we stay one step ahead of our customers? What are the benefits?

Figure 8-1

- How can we stay one step ahead of

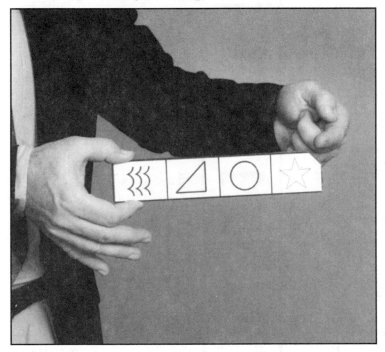

Figure 8-2

our competition? What are the
benefits?

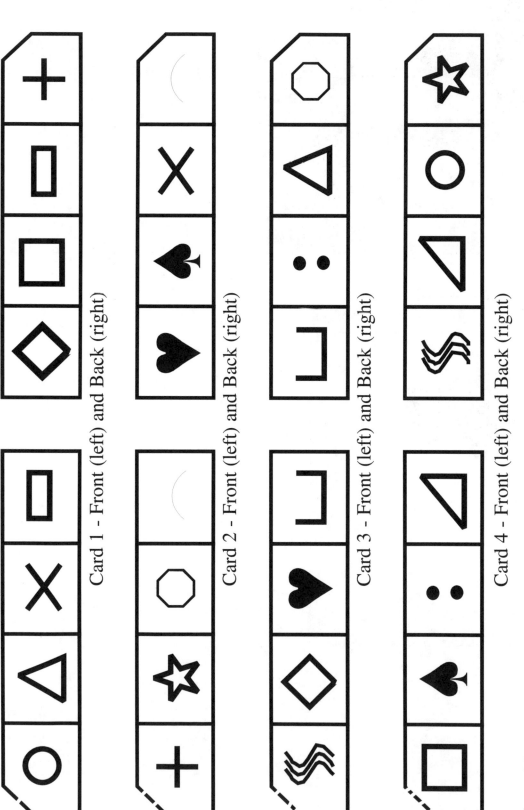

Card 1 - Front (left) and Back (right)

Card 2 - Front (left) and Back (right)

Card 3 - Front (left) and Back (right)

Card 4 - Front (left) and Back (right)

Figure 8-3

Background

This is a quick little exercise that demonstrates the power of the mind. Mental suggestions can actually cause physical reactions.

The Magical Effect

The audience members hold their forefingers apart but parallel to each other. You give them mental suggestions, and, amazingly, their forefingers pull together.

Applying the Magic to Presenting and Training

This is an example of

- the power of the mind,
- the power of positive thinking, and
- the power of visualization.

Because the trick usually does not work for every member of the audience, it can be used to open a discussion on the power of negative thinking. It is also a fun icebreaker.

Materials

- None.

The Trick, Step by Step

Step 1:

Instruct the audience to clasp their hands together and extend their forefingers parallel to each other, about an inch or so apart (Fig. 9-1)

Trick **#9**

The Power of the Mind

In dreams begin reality.

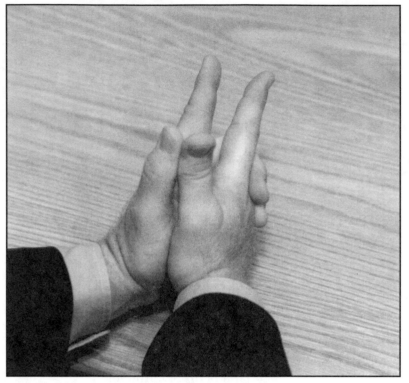

Figure 9-1

For example, some people believe that thinking positively helps them fight deadly diseases. By a show of hands, how many of you believe that? How many of you believe that you can achieve anything if you believe you can? How powerful is the mind? Well, I'd like to try a little experiment to demonstrate the power of the mind." I then instruct them to hold their forefingers parallel to each other. "Please concentrate on your forefingers, and imagine that there is now a tight rubber band around them." *In a firm, deliberate tone,* I repeat, "You can feel the rubber band bringing your fingers closer … closer … closer …." The trick usually works for about two-thirds of the audience, and many people laugh and smile.

Step 2:

Tell the audience to concentrate and imagine that there is a tight rubber band around their forefingers. In a *firm, deliberate tone,* prompt the audience slowly and repeatedly, "You can feel the rubber band bringing your fingers closer … closer … closer …."

Sample Patter

"Positive attitude makes a big difference in many things we do in life.

Debriefing Questions

- Why do you think your fingers moved or did not move?
- What did your imaginary rubber band look like? If your fingers *did not* move, what did you do to counteract the imaginary rubber band?
- Can you give examples when mental suggestions have prompted actions?
- How do attitudes affect teamwork?

Background

This trick dates back to my childhood. Using Magic Principles #2 and #6, I developed this trick to help demonstrate the power of teamwork. I often use this trick at parties to amaze my friends. A motto relevant to this trick is "Working smarter, not harder."

The Magical Effect

Four volunteers lift a fifth volunteer using only their index fingers (Fig. 10-1).

Applying the Magic to Presenting and Training

The trick can be used to demonstrate the power of teamwork. It is also great for opening a discussion on team trust. It can be used to illustrate the benefits of working smarter, not harder. When used at the start of a difficult problem-solving activity, it demonstrates that even a seemingly impossible task can be accomplished if people work together.

Materials

- 1 chair

The Trick, Step by Step

Step 1:

Ask a volunteer to sit on a chair, then ask four volunteers to lift the person off the chair using only their index fingers.

Trick #10

The Power of Teamwork

Teamwork—We didn't all come over on the same ship, but we're all in the same boat.

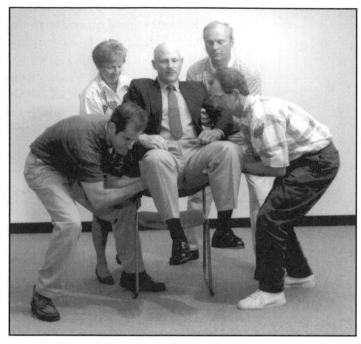

Figure 10-1

Step 2:

Position the four volunteers two on each side of the chair. Have the four volunteers clasp their hands and point their index fingers (Fig. 10-2). Have them place their index fingers under the armpits and knee joints of the seated volunteer, and lift.

On occasion this trick will fail if the lifters are not strong enough. Be-

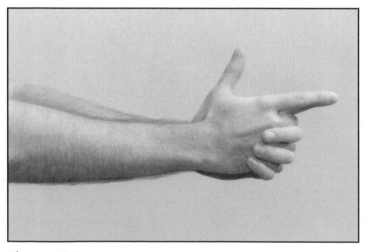

Figure 10-2

cause this is a group exercise more than a magic trick, appropriate debriefing can still make it a valuable learning opportunity.

Note that there is a small possibility of injury. When planning this trick, it's important to consider the physical conditions of the volunteers. Don't try to see how far they can lift the person. Remain flexible if people choose not to participate.

Sample Patter

For the best effect I usually select a relatively big person to be lifted (use good judgment here). If you are a heavyweight like me, you can volunteer yourself! I ask the volunteer to sit in a chair in the middle of the room, then ask the four other volunteers to surround him or her. I ask them, "If I asked any one of you four to lift this person, could you do it? Not likely, and you might even hurt yourself or the person you're lifting. Do you think the four of you together could do the lift?" Most will answer, "Yes." I retort, "With your index fingers? Yes, I want you to try it with just your index fingers. Should be easy, right?" I let them try it, keeping an eye on them for safety reasons. They usually fail, but if they succeed, great! I congratulate them and debrief. If they fail, I tell them that just because they are working simultaneously doesn't mean that they are cooperating. Then I advise, "Let's try something. Think of yourselves as a team now. All good teams need to share tools and techniques in order to be successful. Let me give you some advice from an ancient facilitator, 'Glad the Facilitator.' Here is how to lift a person …." I then show them the proper technique. Before I let them use the technique, however, I tell them, "Before we lift as a team, we must bind the team together. I want you each to put one of your hands, one on top of another, on the volunteer's head. Now close your eyes, take a deep breath, and hold it. Push down on the person's head firmly (but not enough to hurt) and say to yourselves, 'We can lift this person.' **You must believe this in order to do it.** Okay, on the count of six, open your eyes and take up the lifting positions. Then, on the count of three, you will be able to lift the person off the chair with ease." Sometimes the volunteers want to rehearse, and I let them. Once they have completed the lift, I tell them that a team with a positive attitude is hard to beat, and share with them the poem on page 46.

Debriefing Questions

- Why did the team succeed or fail?
- Did you see your group as a team?
- How did you contribute to the team? Whose contribution did you appreciate?
- What role did I (the presenter) play in this exercise?
- Is this really magic? Is teamwork a little like magic?
- How can you relate this exercise to your work?
- Did the power of positive thinking play a role? How does a positive attitude affect the outcome?

The Team Who Think They Can

If we think we are beaten, we are.

If we think we dare not, we don't.

If we like to win, but think we can't,

It's almost a cinch we won't.

If we think we'll lose, we've lost.

For out in this world we find

Success begins with a team's will.

It's all in the state of mind.

If we think we've been outclassed, we are.

We've got to think high to rise.

We've got to be sure of ourselves before

We can ever win a prize.

Life's battles don't always go

To the stronger or faster team,

But sooner or later, the team that succeeds

Is the team that thinks it can.

Background

This trick has been around for a long time and is used by amateurs and professionals alike. Recently I watched "The World's Greatest Magicians" perform a variation of this trick on TV. Used in the right context, this trick will win a lot of fans.

The Magical Effect

After having the audience answer a few simple questions and perform a few simple calculations, you correctly guess that they are thinking of a gray elephant in Denmark!

Applying the Magic to Presenting and Training

This trick demonstrates that you can get the right answers if you ask the right questions. I usually use this in facilitator training classes to illustrate the importance of asking questions instead of giving answers. You can use the trick in a leadership class to open discussions on leadership. It also works well as an icebreaker or after a break. This trick works equally well with large and small groups.

Materials

- A large piece of paper and a pen (optional)

The Trick, Step by Step

Step 1:

Ask everyone in the audience to think of a number between 1 and

---

Trick #**11**

Gray Elephant in Denmark

A "leading authority" is someone who has guessed right more than once.

—*Frank Clark*

10 and apply the following operations to the number in succession:

- Multiply by 2.
- Add 8.
- Divide by 2.
- Subtract the original number from it.

Step 2:

Ask the audience to convert the resulting number to a letter, where A=1, B=2, etc., then think of a European country whose name begins with that letter, a four-legged animal whose name begins with the second letter of that country's name, and the color of that animal.

Step 3:

Ask them to concentrate and transmit their thoughts to you. Act as if you are receiving their thoughts, then exclaim that you are getting a silly message, that there are no gray elephants in Denmark.

The number resulting from Step 1 will always be 4, which converts to D, and Denmark is the only country in Europe that begins with D. It may be helpful to have a large sign posted to help people convert numbers to letters:

1	A
2	B
3	C
4	D
5	E
...	...

There are variations, of course. For example, after having the audience think of Denmark, you could ask them to think of an animal that begins with the last letter of the country's name. Most will think of kangaroo. Then ask them to go to the last letter of the animal's name and think of a fruit that begins with that letter. Most will think of orange. You can conclude, "There are no orange kangaroos in Denmark!" Sometimes a good disguise works with this one for a little tongue-in-cheek humor.

Sample Patter

"I'd like to demonstrate to you that a facilitator doesn't always have to provide answers in order to guide a group. As someone once said, 'If you can ask questions clearly, you are two-thirds of the way toward getting a decent answer.' Sometimes, all you have to do is ask the right questions." After I tell them that there are no gray elephants in Denmark, I conclude, "I've guessed right more than once. Do you know what that means? I'm a leading authority!" The audience starts laughing.

Debriefing Questions

- How many of you had the same answer?
- Why did this happen?
- Did I have the answer from the start?
- How did I lead you to the answer?
- Did you feel as if you were in control of the outcome?
- Are you leading or are you led in this manner at your work?
- What technique are you using to lead others? Can it be less answer-oriented? Explain.

The Structure of Teamwork

Teamwork: Coming together is the beginning; keeping together is progress; working together is success.

—Henry Ford

Background

My father shared this one with me, calling it a "problem puzzle." He would always pick up little tricks like this from his friends and challenge me to solve them. Of course I wasn't able to when I was young, but I never forgot them. This one is a great metaphor for teamwork. A team is only as strong as its weakest link, so helping the weak link will make the team more effective. Remember that each of us has weaknesses and strengths.

The Magical Effect

The audience is challenged to build a structure from four wooden matches and four glasses that can support a fifth glass. After they try, you show them an ingenious solution (Fig. 12-1).

Applying the Magic to Presenting and Training

This exercise works well as a metaphor for teamwork. Each match works off the strength of the other matches; each member relies on the others for support. Because this is a hands-on exercise, it energizes the participants.

Materials

- 5 small glasses (for each team)
- 4 wooden matches (for each team)
- 1 clock

Figure 12-1

Figure 12-2

The Trick, Step by Step

Step 1:

Group the audience into teams and give them the materials. Challenge them to build a structure using the 4 glasses and the 4 matches that will support the fifth glass without the 4 glasses in the base touching each other. The glasses may not touch each other. Time them for 5 minutes.

Step 2:

Demonstrate the solution (Fig. 12-1). The matches must be positioned precisely for them to support a glass (Fig. 12-2).

Be sure to have practiced the solution before the presentation—remember Magic Principle #4. With a small group, it is possible to have people try individually, then try in teams.

Sample Patter

I don't use patter with this trick, but you may want to create one. Give it a try, then write to me and let me know how you used it.

Debriefing Questions

- How did you find the solution?
- What problems were encountered?
- How is this exercise like teamwork?
- How do the matches support a glass?
- How did the time constraint affect your attempt?

Background

Ray Odom, a close friend of mine, used this exercise with the Harris Semiconductor Palm Bay Work Force to demonstrate the power of visualization. I have used it many times in workshops to encourage creating a vision for oneself. This little demonstration of the power of the mind can be used to prepare for a more strenuous exercise of the power of the mind, "The Power of Teamwork" (Trick #10).

The Magical Effect

The audience is asked to note how far they can twist their upper bodies. After they are guided through a visualization exercise, they surprise themselves by twisting far past their previous positions.

Applying the Magic to Presenting and Training

This exercise is relevant to many topics: power of visualization, power of positive thinking, importance of having goals or a vision. It can be used with either small or large groups, but is especially fun when a large audience participates.

Materials

- None

The Trick, Step by Step

Step 1:

Instruct the audience to stand and spread out so that they have plen-

---

#13

Let's Do the Twist

First you form your habits, then they form you.

—*Socrates*

Figure 13-1

ty of room to move their arms. Instruct them to raise their right arms to a right angle to their bodies, point their index fingers stright ahead at the wall in front of them (fig. 13-1) and rotate their torsos with their outstrecthed arms clockwise as far as they can without moving their feet (13-2). Be sure to demonstrate this, as in the photos, while you instruct the audience. When they've reached as far as they can comfortably reach, ask them to take note of how far they rotated by sighting a spot on the wall, then return to a comfortable straight position and relax.

Figure 13-2

Step 2:

Ask them to close their eyes and visualize themselves rotating their torsos to the point where they stopped previously, then past that point by 20 percent. Ask them to visualize returning to a comfortable straight position and relax. Repeat the visualization sequence, turning 30 percent past the first point. Repeat the visualization sequence, turning 50 percent past the first point.

Step 3:

Ask the audience to open their eyes and rotate their torsos clockwise as far as possible and compare the result with their first try.

What's the secret, you ask? Sorry, but the Zen master told me never to tell anybody. Maybe this is not actually an illusion or a trick, but a real example of the power of visualization. What do you think?

Sample Patter

I begin by explaining to the audience that I am going to walk them through an exercise that demonstrates the power of visualization. When asked to raise their right arms, some undoubtedly raise their left arms and I give them the old, "No, your *other* right arm!" I tell them to raise their arms as if they were sighting down a rifle barrel. Before the visualization step, I stress that we must not be self-conscious, that we must let ourselves be a little silly and delay evaluation until the entire exercise is finished. Most people are amazed at how much farther they can go past their initial try.

Debriefing Questions

- What do you think happened?
- Does visualizing a result help you obtain that result?
- Can you think of a way to improve something in your life by visualizing better results?
- Has visualization helped you in the past?

Background

It takes a big stretch of the imagination to say this one is a magic trick. I include it here for two reasons: it effectively demonstrates the importance of listening and it's an excellent way to feel the power of misdirection that is so important in magic tricks. This trick is as much for you as it is for your audience.

The Magical Effect

You tell a simple story and hand some coins to a volunteer. Misdirected by the coins, the volunteer is unable to answer a simple question about the story.

Jenny's Mother Had Three Children

We have two ears and one mouth so we should listen twice as much as we speak.

—*Lou Holtz, Football Coach, Notre Dame*

Applying the Magic to Presenting and Training

This is a perfect exercise for discussions on listening. It also demonstrates the power of visual distractions. It is a fun icebreaker too.

Materials

- 1 nickel
- 1 dime

The Trick, Step by Step

Step 1:

Ask a volunteer to hold one hand open and listen.

Step 2:

Playfully recite the ditty below. As you say "nickel," place a nickel in the volunteer's palm. As you say "dime," place a dime in the volunteer's palm.

You must draw the audience's attention to the coins using the tone of your voice and by exaggerating your hand motion as you place the coins. When you ask, "What was the third child's name?" most people will answer "Quarter." The correct is, of course, "Jenny." Be sure to have "Jenny's Mom Had Three Children" memorized:

> Jenny's mom had three children,
> First one was named Nickel,
> Second one was named Dime.
> What was the third child's name?

Sample Patter

Some people answer correctly, but most do not. If a volunteer gives the right answer, I respond, "Good job, are you a good listener or have you seen this before?" I also ask the audience how many of them had the correct answer. If they don't get the answer, I may go through the trick again, being cautious not to go over it too many times. I try to sense whether the volunteer is embarrassed or frustrated and make sure not to damage the self-esteem of the volunteer.

Debriefing Questions

- What did I do to distract you? What drew your attention? What role did the nickel and dime play?

- What makes a good listener? Can you tell us an interesting story about listening? How is listening important in your work? How can we improve our listening skills?

- How do you define a gossip, a bore, and a brilliant conversationalist? A gossip is one who talks to you about others; a bore is someone who talks to you about himself; and a brilliant conversationalist is one who talks to you about yourself.

Background

This is a variation of a trick David Copperfield performed on television. When you do this one you can brag that you have done the same tricks as David Copperfield. Of course, this one has a little different twist. This trick provides an excellent opportunity for you to create your own patter.

The Magical Effect

You guide a volunteer's steps around a wheel of symbols, based on a secretly chosen number. You name the correct destination without ever having looked at the symbols.

Applying the Magic to Presenting and Training

I use this exercise to symbolize expertise and to stress the importance of knowing your system thoroughly. It is also useful for broaching a discussion on effective communication. It is an entertaining trick, so it works well as an icebreaker.

Materials

- Overhead projector
- Transparency of the wheel of symbols (Fig. 15-1)
- 1 felt-tip pen

Alternatively, you can draw a copy of the wheel of symbols on a large piece of paper or on a chalkboard.

Trick #**15**

Wheel of Symbols

Failures are divided into two categories—those who thought and never did, and those who did and never thought.

The Trick, Step by Step

Step 1:

Project the wheel of symbols, and stand with your back to the projector and the projection. Have a volunteer stand next to the projector. Give the volunteer the felt-tip pen and ask him or her to pick a number between five and fifteen, without revealing it.

Step 2:

Instruct the volunteer to start at the Start symbol and move as many symbols counter-clockwise as the chosen number. The Start symbol itself should not be counted but the Arrow symbols should be counted for this step. Ask the volunteer to cross off the two Arrow symbols and the Start symbol and ignore them for the remainder of the exercise. Tell the volunteer to move the same number of symbols clockwise around the wheel.

Step 3:

Announce that you know that Symbol #12 is not the currently chosen symbol, and ask the volunteer to cross off symbol #12 and ignore it. Do the same with Symbols #6, #4, and #8.

Step 4:

Have the volunteer move four symbols in either direction, with a reminder to skip over the crossed-off symbols.

Step 5:

Announce that you know that Symbol #11 is not the currently chosen symbol, and ask the volunteer to cross off symbol #11 and ignore it. Do the same with Symbols #2 and #10.

Step 6:

Announce to the audience that the volunteer is on Symbol #3, and confirm with the volunteer.

If the steps are followed correctly, the volunteer will always land on Symbol #3.

Sample Patter

This is a very basic trick but David Copperfield made it seem like the miracle of the century. Entertaining patter and lively acting distract the audience from thinking about the mechanics of this trick. I take my time announcing the symbols to cross off, pretending that I am engaged in deep thought in selecting the symbols to cross off. I occasionally make a mistake, but that's okay: To get maximum attention, it's hard to beat a big mistake by the magician!

Figure 15-1

Background

I learned this trick from Mary Jo Pennino of Tampa Electric while attending a workshop. I modified it and used it successfully in my workshops and presentations. It's simple and audiences like it.

The Magical Effect

A volunteer is shown 6 cards, each with 32 numbers on them. The volunteer is asked to pick out the cards that contain his or her age, and afterward you tell the correct age.

Applying the Magic to Presenting and Training

I use the magic cards as business cards; I put my name and phone number on the back and give them out after performing the trick. The cards can be given to business contacts and friends. The trick makes a special impression on people. Recently I taught the trick to physical education teachers and customized the cards for them (Fig. 16-1). The teachers performed the trick for their students and gave the cards to them.

Materials

- The 6 cards in Figure 16-1

The back of the cards can be customized for your presentation, but the front (the numbers) must be replicated exactly. I recommend that you laminate the cards.

Trick #16
The Age Teller

Don't worry about the world coming to an end today because it's already tomorrow in Australia.

The Trick, Step by Step

Step 1:

Select a volunteer and give these instructions: "Say yes if I show you a card with your age on it; otherwise say no."

Step 2:

Hand the cards to the volunteer slowly, one at a time. The volunteer's age is the sum of the top-left numbers on all cards that contain his or her age.

The magic is more convincing the less time you spend handling the cards. Try to add up the numbers as you go through the cards with the volunteer, instead of examining the stack afterwards. If you make a mistake adding the numbers or want to double check, just go through the routine again (invent and announce a creative excuse to the audience).

If revealing someone's age to the audience seems inappropriate, ask the volunteer to choose a number between 1 and 63 instead.

Sample Patter

I announce to the audience, "By looking at these cards I can tell your age!" I may discuss the writing on the back of the cards as the volunteer and I go through the cards—this adds a little distraction to the trick and also helps reinforce the lesson of the presentation. Before I guess the age of the volunteer, I add a little acting by saying, "I'm getting a strong feeling that your number is..."

Note: This trick only works for people 63 or younger. With a more mature audience you should use the "choose a number ..." patter instead.

4 5 6 7 12 13 14 15 20 21 22 23 28 29 30 31 36 37 38 39 44 45 46 47 52 53 54 55 60 61 62 63	**Thinking is like living and dying, each of us must do it for ourselves.** *- Unknown*
32 33 34 35 36 37 38 39 40 41 42 43 44 45 46 47 48 49 50 51 52 53 54 55 56 57 58 59 60 61 62 63	**RESPECT YOURSELF.** *Respect others.*
16 17 18 19 20 21 22 23 24 25 26 27 28 29 30 31 48 49 50 51 52 53 54 55 56 57 58 59 60 61 62 63	**The difference between the impossible and the possible lies in a person's determination.** *- Tommy Lasorda*
2 3 6 7 10 11 14 15 18 19 22 23 26 27 30 31 34 35 38 39 42 43 46 47 50 51 54 55 58 59 62 63	**BE POSITIVE.** *A good attitude is a key to your future.*
8 9 10 11 12 13 14 15 24 25 26 27 28 29 30 31 40 41 42 43 44 45 46 47 56 57 58 59 60 61 62 63	**Why do we do what we do when we know what we know?** *- Dennis Waitley* **THINK** before you **ACT**
1 3 5 7 9 11 13 15 17 19 21 23 25 27 29 31 33 35 37 39 41 43 45 47 49 51 53 55 57 59 61 63	**We have two ears and one mouth so we should listen twice as much as we talk.** *- Lou Holtz*

Figure 16-1

#17
Roman Finger Test

If there's a better way to do it ... find it.
—*Thomas Edison*

Background

My grandfather used this trick in local pubs for laughs. I adapted it for use in ending facilitator training classes, with hilarious results.

The Magical Effect

Everyone is asked to place their right hands on a table and asked to raise a particular finger in response to your questions. After responding to several routine questions, they are asked a pointed question and they cannot lift the designated finger no matter how hard they try.

Applying the Magic to Presenting and Training

I use it at the end of training classes to send the students out with a smile. It is a lighthearted way to end any presentation while remaining relevant to the theme of the presentation. The questions I use can easily be modified for any presentation. With appropriate questions this trick should work well as an icebreaker.

Materials

- None

The Trick, Step by Step

Step 1:

Instruct the audience to place their right hands on a flat surface with all fingers except the middle finger outstretched. The middle finger should be curled, with its

63

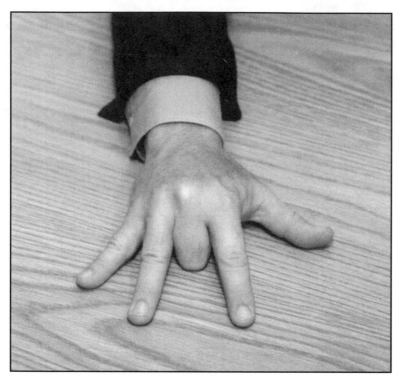

Figure 17-1

Sample Patter

"Well, I'd like to conclude today's class with a test. It will tell us whether you are prepared to work as a facilitator. The test was handed down to me through many generations. My grandfather told me it comes from an ancient Roman emperor. Although I can't verify that, I've never known my grandfather to lie. Well, you can judge for yourself the validity of the test." Making sure that everyone's hand is positioned correctly, I ask the first question: "Are you planning to be a facilitator? If so, raise your right thumb." Most people raise their thumbs. The second question is: "Do you think this will be an interesting job? If so, raise your pinky." Pinkies go up. My third question is: "Do you think you will enjoy working as a facilitator? If so, raise your index finger." Most people raise their index fingers.

Then I prime the audience for the finale. "How valid is this test so far? Do you think my grandfather was right? Well, let's do the final question." Again, making sure that everyone's hands are in correct position, I say, "So far your fingers have told the truth. Please continue to be honest. Do you think you will be good at your job? If so, raise your ring finger."

If everyone is enjoying the trick, I ask one more question: "Do you think my grandfather told me the truth about the test? If so, raise your ring finger."

knuckle resting on the flat surface (Fig. 17-1).

Step 2:

Ask the audience a routine question, and ask them to raise their thumbs if they want to answer yes. Repeat using the pinky and the index finger. Be sure to ask questions to which most people will answer yes.

Step 3:

Ask a question that must be answered with a yes, and ask the volunteers to raise their ring fingers in response.

The physiology of the human hand prevents the ring finger from being lifted when the middle finger is curled. The real secret of this trick is good patter.

Background

An associate shared this trick with me a few years back. I framed it as a problem-solving exercise, because restating the problem makes it easy to solve. Or, should I say, *easier* to solve.

The Magical Effect

Volunteers are challenged to balance a glass on a sheet of paper, which in turn must rest on two glasses. The glasses are not allowed to touch each other nor directly support each other. After ten minutes, you restate the problem, which makes the solution plain.

Applying the Magic to Presenting and Training

This exercise is pertinent to any presentation related to problem solving. It shows that restating a difficult problem often leads to plain solutions. This exercise is also relevant to team-building workshops and leadership classes—a leader must have innovative perspectives. You may run the exercise with individuals, teams, or both.

Materials

- 3 small glasses
- One 8½″ × 11″ sheet of paper

The Trick, Step by Step

Step 1:

Tell the volunteers that they must balance a glass on a sheet of paper, which in turn must be

#18

Restate the Problem (Balancing Glass)

We cannot direct the wind but we can adjust our sails.

balanced on two glasses. The glasses may not touch each other nor can they directly support each other. Give them 10 minutes to find a solution.

Step 2:

Restate the challenge by asking them how they can fold the sheet of paper so that it can support a glass. Give them 5 minutes to find a solution. If they still cannot find a solution, tell them to fanfold the paper (Fig. 18-1).

You may fill the top glass with water to make the challenge appear more difficult. Be prepared for a soggy workshop!

Debriefing Questions

- How difficult did the problem seem to you?

- What were your initial solutions to the problem? Did you consider folding the paper?

- Would the problem have seemed difficult if the challenge emphasized the paper instead of the glasses?

- In your work, do you restate problems?

- What did you gain by working together as a team?

Figure 18-1

Background

This trick is based on the "triple backup" concept: You prepare for all possible outcomes. I've successfully customized this trick for training classes for salespeople using Magic Principle #6. The props are especially easy to prepare, so I customize them for each occasion.

The Magical Effect

You announce that you have already predicted which one of three cards a volunteer would choose. After the volunteer chooses one you show proof that you correctly predicted the choice.

Applying the Magic to Presenting and Training

I use this trick at the end of a presentation on personality types. I boast that I got to know the volunteer so well during the presentation that I can predict the volunteer's card choice. The trick is also a very simple icebreaker for business meetings. You can joke that the trick demonstrates how well you understand each other.

Materials

- 1 green card, 1 blue card, 1 red card (you can just put colored stickers on white cards). Write on the back of the green card, "You will choose the green card."
- 1 envelope containing a piece of paper that says, "You will choose the blue card."

| Trick **#19** |

The Triple Backup

The best way to predict the future is to create it.
—*Stephen Covey*

- 1 business card, the back of which says, "You will choose the red card."

There are many options for preparing the materials. For example, it is relatively inexpensive to get a pen inscribed with "You will choose the red card."

The Trick, Step by Step

Step 1:

Ask a volunteer to select one of the three cards. After the volunteer chooses one, offer repeated chances to change the selection. You want the audience to think that you want the volunteer to select a different card.

Step 2:

If the volunteer chooses the green card, flip it over and show it to the audience. If the volunteer chooses the blue card, take out the prepared envelope from your pocket and show the paper inside it to the audience. If the volunteer chooses

the red card, take out the prepared business card and show it to the audience.

Sample Patter

"We have been discussing the Meyers-Briggs test, and I would like to demonstrate its effectiveness. While we were using the test today, I have gotten to know each one of you very well." I ask for a volunteer, and after selecting one, I say, "I'm glad you volunteered because I know you have a helpful personality." Laying out the three cards, I announce that I have already predicted which card the volunteer will choose. I ask the volunteer to choose one. When the volunteer chooses one, I look very concerned, and ask the volunteer to be sure about the choice. Whether or not the volunteer changes the selection, I ask again if this is the final choice. Then I reveal the appropriate prop predicting the choice, and quickly continue with the presentation.

Background

This is an old trick that I customized into a metaphor for change.

The Magical Effect

You push a large needle through a balloon without popping it, then pop the balloon using the same needle.

Applying the Magic to Presenting and Training

You may use this trick as a metaphor for change, as I do in the Sample Patter. It is appropriate for any presentation addressing difficult changes.

Materials

- Several 11″ transparent balloons
- One 18″ needle
- 1 case for the needle
- Petroleum jelly

Balloons may be purchased at a party store or a general retailer. Buy the thickest balloons available. The needle must be sharp. The needle case should be filled with petroleum jelly so that the needle is already coated with jelly when you pull it out to use it. You can make your own needle and case, but it's easier to just buy a set from a magic shop (see the list of magic shops at the back of the book).

The Trick, Step by Step

Step 1:

Balloons are thickest at the neck and the top. Slowly but firmly in-

Needle through a Balloon

Only those who have the patience to do simple things perfectly acquire the skill to do difficult things easily.

Unknown

sert the needle at the base and push through to the top. Twist the needle as you push.

Step 2:

Pull the needle out. Toss the balloon into the air and pop it with the tip of the needle.

Sample Patter

At the end of a workshop for managing change in organizations, I say to the audience, "Here is a balloon—let's think of it as an organization. And think of this eighteen-inch needle as change that the organization faces. Do you think I can take this eighteen-inch needle and insert it through the balloon without breaking the balloon?" Many in the audience will shake their heads and reply, "No way." I continue, "Change can really rupture an organization, but what if I seek out experts? I can observe their methods for implementing change, ask about pitfalls, and invest in proper tools. I should be able to insert the needle into the balloon without breaking it." I then proceed to insert the needle into the balloon (Fig. 20-1).

Figure 20-1

After the needle is inserted, I remark, "I don't know of anything more fragile than a balloon, but with the proper preparations anything is possible. The same applies to implementing change in an organization." I then pull the needle through the balloon. To end the trick with a bang, I pop the balloon with the needle.

This trick is not guaranteed to work every time. The balloon sometimes breaks, regardless of my preparation. If it breaks, I say, "This is just like making changes in organizations. Even when you've done everything exactly right, you'll be faced with some surprises and have to improvise." I've found this to be as effective as successfully getting the needle through the balloon.

Background

Thanks to Chuck Palmer, who shared this with me. He is the Director of Product Engineering at Harris Semiconductor. This knotty trick probably originated in the Navy. It's a powerful argument for the need for out-of-the-box thinking, a need for new approaches to old problems.

The Magical Effect

A volunteer is challenged to tie a simple knot without letting go of the rope. You show them that the secret begins with the approach.

Applying the Magic to Presenting and Training

I use this trick in a Lateral Thinking workshop to help participants visualize their lesson. It shows how being tied to old paradigms can limit our problem-solving abilities. This trick works with many volunteers if you provide rope for everyone.

Trick #21

The Knotty Challenge

Everyone is a prisoner of their own experience.

Materials

One 20″ piece of rope for each volunteer

If using many volunteers, you may want to substitute inexpensive string for rope.

The Trick, Step by Step

Step 1:

Demonstrate a simple overhand knot (Fig. 21-1).

Step 2:

Untie your knot, then lay the rope straightened out on a table. Instruct the volunteer to tie an overhand knot. Neither hand may let go of the rope after the volunteer grabs the rope (Fig. 21-2). Allow the volunteer 10 minutes to solve the problem.

Step 3:

Demonstrate the solution: Cross your arms and pick up each end of the rope (Fig. 21-3). As you unfold your arms the knot is tied (Fig. 21-4).

Sample Patter

After I lay the rope on a table, I like to tell the volunteer, "Pretend you have super-glue on your fingers, and it won't allow you to let go once you touch the ends of the rope." I encourage each volunteer to solve the problem with no help from others. When doing this in teams, many solve it by having one person grab each end of the rope. I applaud this solution but tell them it's not the correct solution—one person must tie the rope. I may respond, "That's a good idea, but the customer won't accept that method per the specifications."

Some may complain that this is a trick. I tell them they're right—it's a trick that can only be solved if we think differently from the way we've been trained to tie knots. There may be solutions to this trick other than the one I told you. This trick is about paradigms so I make sure I'm not tied to one; I remain open to other solutions. Joel Barker, a futurist, says, "It's best to have paradigm flexibility versus paradigm paralysis."

Debriefing Questions

- Did you think this was an impossible task?
- How did you approach the problem? What solutions did you try?
- How did you succeed?
- Are there problems at your workplace that can use a fresh approach?

Figure 21-1

Figure 21-2

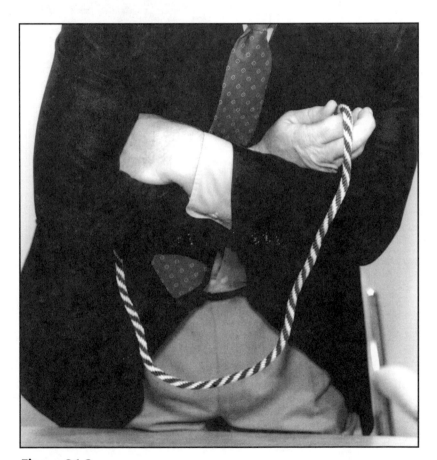

Figure 21-3

Figure 21-4

Background

I learned this trick at a magic convention and have used it successfully as a humorous icebreaker. It's tongue-in-cheek magic.

The Magical Effect

To the volunteer it appears that you made a napkin disappear in your hand, but the audience can see plainly that you merely threw it behind the volunteer.

Applying the Magic to Presenting and Training

This trick can be used as an icebreaker for a training class.

Materials

- 1 paper napkin
- 1 chair

You may substitute anything light and small for the paper napkin. It must not make a sound when it hits the floor.

The Trick, Step by Step

Step 1:

Have a volunteer sit on a chair in front of the audience, facing the audience. Stand on the volunteer's left.

Step 2:

Hold your left palm in front of the volunteer's face and show a napkin, tightly balled, with your right hand (Fig. 22-1). Tell the volunteer to keep focused on the napkin.

Trick #**22**

Vanishing Napkin

Before you give someone a piece of your mind,

make sure you can get by with what you have left.

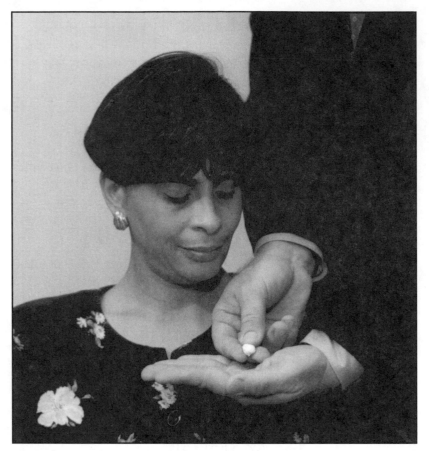

Figure 22-1

Step 3:

Raise your right hand three times, pivoting at the wrist, out of the volunteer's sight (Fig. 22-2). On the third time toss the napkin behind the volunteer. Show your right hand to the volunteer (Fig. 22-3).

It is essential to keep the volunteer's attention on your left palm. Raise your right hand quickly and smoothly so that the volunteer cannot turn to follow it.

Sample Patter

Because this is a silly trick, I try to set a silly atmosphere at every opportunity. "Before we start today, I think it's important for me to demonstrate some of my magical abilities. Would you like to see a great magic trick? Well, so would I, but we'll have to settle for the one I had planned! Could one of you help me? Thanks." After seating the volunteer in front of the audience, I ask, "What's your name?" When the person answers I reply, "That's right! You see, I don't ask hard questions in this class."

Standing next to the volunteer, I ask, "Now, for the second greatest magic trick, please focus on the middle of my hand and I'll show you something that you may never forget. Now, do you see this napkin? Please focus on it." I raise my right hand twice and after each time ask the volunteer to keep focusing on the napkin. After the third time (after I've tossed the napkin behind the volunteer), I show my empty right hand and say, "Isn't that the best trick you've ever seen? You might all be thinking, 'What's that got to do with our class today?' Well, just like the trick, if you don't pay close attention something may just go right over your head today. So let's have some fun and let's get started."

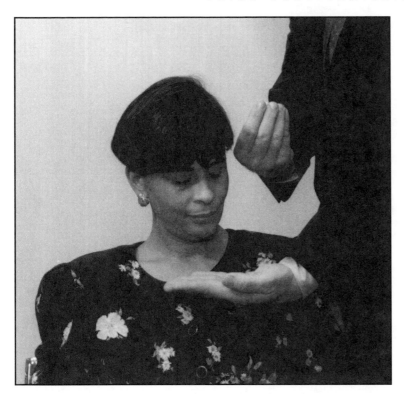

Figure 22-2

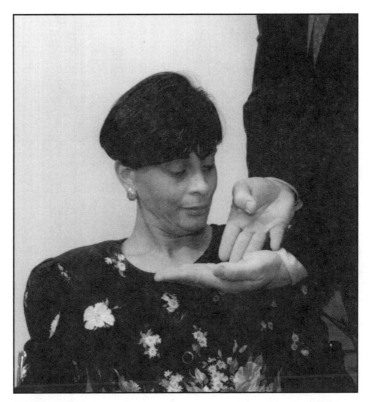

Figure 22-3

Background

This is a recreational puzzle from 1929. It is a great example of the importance of looking at things from different angles.

The Magical Effect

Teams of volunteers are given puzzles to put together in 5 minutes. The puzzles consist of only four pieces, but the task is unexpectedly difficult.

Applying the Magic to Presenting and Training

You may use this puzzle to simulate competition and cooperation among teams within a company. It can illustrate the importance of looking at problems from different angles. It also works well as an icebreaker.

The Magic T

If all you've been trained with is a hammer, then the whole world looks like a nail!

Materials

- 1 puzzle per team
- 1 envelope per team
- 1 table per team

Follow Figure 23-1 to cut a copy of Figure 23-2 into puzzle pieces. Place one set of puzzle pieces in each envelope.

The Trick, Step by Step

Step 1:

Separate the audience into teams and position each team around a table.

Step 2:

Give each team a puzzle, and tell them they have 5 minutes to form a T out of the pieces.

Sample Patter

I use this exercise to simulate competition within a company. I ask each team to create a team name, and position them around separate tables. I ask each team to select a representative, and hold a meeting with them (we are competing but we belong to the same company, so a meeting is appropriate), where I give them the puzzles. I tell them we have to solve this problem in 5 minutes to help the profit picture for the year. Because this is a simulation, I purposely refrain from spelling out detailed rules. I want the volunteers to simulate their work behavior. Teams seldom benchmark or cooperate with other teams, because most think that is cheating. The cheating paradigm comes from our school days and may not always be appropriate for competition within a company. Because the T is cut at weird angles, only about half of the teams working independently solve the puzzle. When teams work together, however, I've never had a team fail.

I may complement this exercise with "The Knotty Challenge" (Trick #21) and give them 10 minutes to solve both puzzles.

Debriefing Questions

- Did you work as a team?
- Did you work with other teams?
- How did you define the team—the company, or your team only?
- Did you recognize the pre-meeting as a company meeting?
- Did you do any benchmarking with the other, internal teams? Why or why not?

Magic 'T' Puzzle
(Four pieces total)

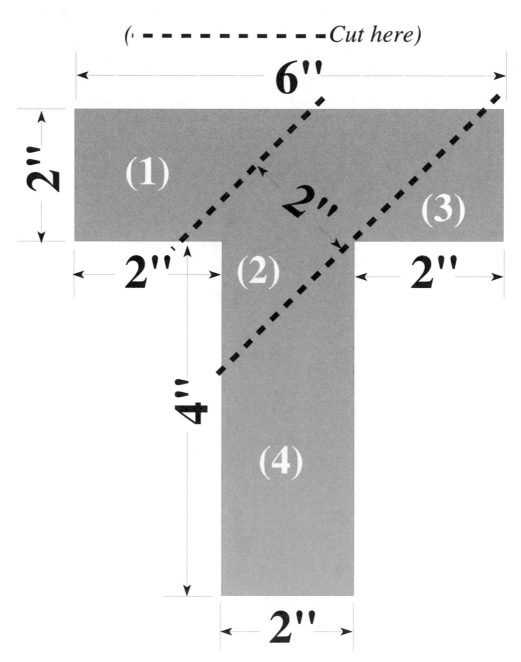

Figure 23-1

Figure 23-2

#24

What Is Synergy?

Teamwork: Coming together is the beginning; keeping together is progress; working together is success.

—*Henry Ford*

Background

This is a classic rope trick invented by Edward Victor, a notable English magician. It's magic—pure and simple. It is performed by many professional magicians but it's unlikely that any of them have performed the trick with the patter I share below. Using the Seven Magic Principles, I developed this trick into a metaphor for synergy. Although this trick does take some practice, the secret is really very simple. Try it and you'll love it!

The Magical Effect

You pick up three pieces of rope of different lengths (Fig. 24-1). When you hold them together, they have transformed into three pieces of equal length (Fig. 24-2). You show each transformed piece (Fig. 24-3), then tie them together and again show that they are equal in length (Fig. 24-4).

Applying the Magic to Presenting and Training

I use this trick as a metaphor for the synergy that occurs in teamwork: Team members help each other, and the whole becomes greater than the sum of its parts.

Materials

- One 11″ piece of rope
- One 22″ piece of rope
- One 36″ piece of rope

The three pieces of rope must be of the same color and diameter.

The Trick, Step by Step

The ropes are labeled with letters for this explanation. When performing in front of an audience, of course, the ropes should not be labeled.

Step 1:

Hold the three ropes apart to show that they are different lengths (Fig. 24-1).

Step 2:

Hold one end of each of the three ropes in your left hand (Fig. 24-5), letting the audience see only the back of your left hand. Bring the other end of the ropes up to your left hand one at a time (Fig. 24-6). Pull down one end of the middle-length rope (E) then pull down *both* ends of the longest rope (C, F) (Fig. 24-7) so that the rope hangs on the shortest rope (Fig. 24-8). The ropes should appear to be equal in length to the audience (Fig. 24-2).

Step 3:

Pull the middle-length rope by the upper end (B) out of your hand and show that it is whole (Fig. 24-3), then put it back in your left hand. Tug on the bottom of another rope (actually the other two ends belong to the same rope, the longest rope), then pull the middle-length rope out again, pretending that this is another rope. Repeat one more time, tugging on the bottom of the "third" rope.

Step 4:

Bring up one end (F) the longest rope and tie it to the upper end (B) of the middle-length rope. Tie the shortest rope tightly around the middle of the longest rope. Show the connected ropes to the audience. It should appear that three equal-length ropes are tied together (Fig. 24-4).

You should be able to perform this trick smoothly after some practice. If you have any problems with it, please write or visit your local magic shop and ask for help. Most magic shops are staffed by very friendly people who enjoy helping a new magician.

Sample Patter

As I pick up the three ropes and show them to the audience (Step 1) I say, "I have here 'Employee A,' 'Employee B,' and 'Employee C.' They are all different, aren't they? Just as team members that come together, they are all different. Each brings strengths and weaknesses to the team. On a team, if you pull together and use each other's strengths, the entire team will be more productive and create synergy." After I have transformed the ropes into equal lengths (Steps 3), I say, "When team members work together, each member becomes stronger." As I show the ropes tied together (Step 4), I say, "This is synergy, when the whole is greater than the sum of the parts."

Figure 24-1

Figure 24-2

Figure 24-3

Figure 24-4

Figure 24-5

Figure 24-6

Figure 24-7

Figure 24-8

What's Your Name?

You know you're in a bad situation when the best thing that can happen to you is for you to live with your mistake.

Background

My good friend Harry Johnson taught me this trick. I used the Magic Principles to develop my own patter.

The Magical Effect

A volunteer selects nine cards from a deck of cards. You have the volunteer lay down as many cards as there are letters in his or her name, and then repeat using your name. You are then able to predict which card the volunteer chose.

Applying the Magic to Presenting and Training

This trick can be used to demonstrate the need for developing a smart system or illustrate the importance of having a watertight plan for production. You can use it to launch a discussion on establishing a system of controls.

Materials

- 1 deck of cards

Standard playing cards work fine, but you may want to make your own cards with pictures and words relevant to your presentation. The volunteer needs to be able to randomly select only 9 cards for the trick, so 15 to 20 customized cards will suffice.

The Trick, Step by Step

Step 1:

Select a volunteer and ask his or her name.

Step 2:

Ask the volunteer to select 9 cards out of the deck. Ask the volunteer to hold the cards like a fan and memorize the eighth card from the left. Ask the volunteer to hold the cards in a stack again.

Step 3:

If the volunteer's name consists of 5 letters, ask him or her to spell the name, putting a card down into a stack for each letter. The cards should be put face down. If the volunteer's name is not 5 letters long, ask him or her to spell an appropriate 5-letter word (e.g., "smart"). Ask the volunteer to put the remaining cards on top of the stack.

Step 4:

Ask the volunteer to spell your name, putting a card down for each letter. If your name is not 5 letters long, have the volunteer spell the first name of that famous magician, Edwin Rose.

Step 5:

Announce that the first three cards are not what the volunteer chose, and ask the volunteer to flip them over. Repeat with the next two cards. Repeat with the next one card. Announce that the next card is the chosen card and ask the volunteer to flip it over.

Sample Patter

At a presentation concerning manufacturing processes I may begin, "I would like someone to help me demonstrate the value of having a smart system." I explain that a smart system has the knowledge to help workers, and that this is an example of such a system. "This process is a smart system—it knows what it going to happen according to what has happened so far. This system even recognizes names, as you will see! A smart system like this one can help manufacturing operators at various steps in production."

For a presentation related to human resources, I use cards with words describing human behavior written on them: Trust, Faith, Fairness, Equality, Encouragement, Dignity, Courage, Kindness, Modesty, Patience, Potential, Appearance, Clarity, and Communication. The patter is customized too, of course.

Trick #26

Mind Reading Made Simple

If you can't tell the difference, what difference does it make?

—*Unknown*

Background

I learned this trick from my son, Scott, who told me one day he could read minds, and proceeded to demonstrate his ability. It seemed like real magic despite its simplicity. The best magic is the simplest. Remember, it's the story you wrap around a trick that makes the trick seem like a miracle.

The Magical Effect

A volunteer shuffles a deck of cards, places them in a glass, then takes the first card. Without seeing the face of the card, you identify it.

Applying the Magic to Presenting and Training

I've used this fun trick as an ice-breaker to begin a day of technical workshops. You should be able to relate this trick to many subjects using good patter. I encourage you to innovate!

Materials

- 1 deck of cards
- 1 glass
- 1 very small mirror (A dental mirror can be used. You can buy it in any drugstore.)

The Trick, Step by Step

Step 1:

Secretly place a small mirror on the inside of a ring finger (Fig. 26-1).

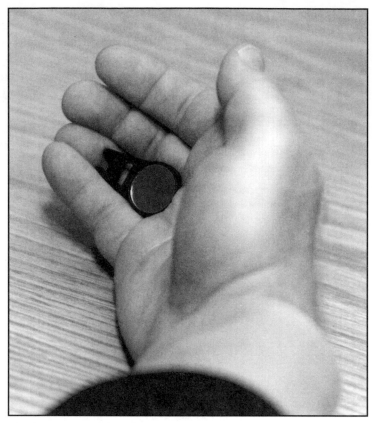

Figure 26-1

Step 2:

Have a volunteer shuffle a deck of cards and place them vertically in a glass. The cards should face away from you.

Step 3:

Holding the glass with both hands, use the mirror to read the first card (Fig. 26-2). Ask a volunteer to take away the first card, then you announce what card it was.

Sample Patter

I begin the story, "When I was in Tibet during my summer vaca-tion,"—I'm making this up—"I developed a close relationship with one of the high priests, whom they call lamas. He told me that if I practiced I could read minds. I studied under him for several months. Today in class I'm not going to read minds because it may not work. Then again, it may work and you or I may be embarrassed. I'm going to use a deck of cards and this glass." I give the cards and the glass to the audience and ask them to examine them to make sure that they are normal. I have a volunteer shuffle the deck of cards and place them in the glass.

Holding the glass with both hands, I tell the audience that, as instructed by the lama, I need to concentrate and feel the closeness with the cards, to be one with the cards. When a volunteer is taking away the first card, I may dramatize the moment by turning my head so as not to see the card. Before I tell which card it was, I mention that the audience has seen for themselves that the cards and the glass are normal. I often mind read a few more cards to make an impact, but stop before I lose their attention.

I close by saying that the subject of the workshop today may seem difficult to some, as learning to read must have been. I assure them that just as I learned to mind read they will grasp today's materials with a little effort.

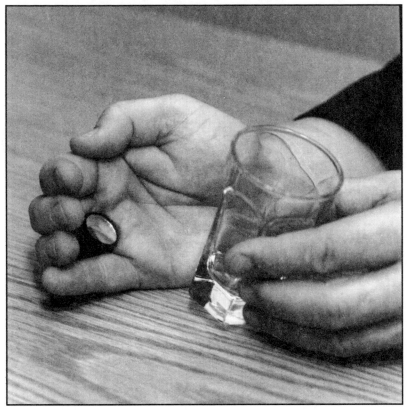

Figure 26-2

Background

I picked this one up from my friend, Doyle Kropff. It has great potential but it's also challenging to perform well. Be sure to develop good patter that matches your style.

The Magical Effect

Seven volunteers each write the name of a living relative on cards. One volunteer writes the name of a deceased relative on a card. After mixing the cards, you can tell by reading the names which ones are living and which is dead.

Applying the Magic to Presenting and Training

I've used this trick to start a workshop on setting up *key monitors* within a manufacturing environment. I emphasize that I make my predictions using a *key monitor*—the power of the living. This trick could be used to demonstrate the importance of a control system. I am confident that any magic trick can be made relevant and effective with the right story.

Materials

- 7 #2 pencils
- 1 #3 pencil
- 8 business cards
- 1 bowl or hat (large enough to hold the cards)

Note: All 8 pencils should look identical.

Trick #27

The Power of the Living

Any significant breakthrough was first started with a break from the past.

—Stephen Covey

The Trick, Step by Step

Step 1:

Ask seven volunteers each to write the name of a living relative on the back of a business card. Ask one volunteer to write the name of a deceased relative on the back of a business card. Give the pencils and the cards to the volunteers. Be sure to give the #3 pencil to the one who is to write the name of a deceased relative.

Step 2:

Collect the cards in a bowl and mix them. Read the names one by one and tell whether each is living or dead. Because #2 pencils write darker than #3 pencils, the darker names are the living relatives and the lighter one is the deceased relative. You may need to hold the cards like a fan and compare the darkness of the writing.

Sample Patter

My work is done when I hand out the pencils, so at other times I work to add misdirection. I don't look at the people writing on the cards, nor do I handle the cards going into the bowl. When I identify the living and the dead, I say that I'm able to do this because of the power that flows from the living.

It's always important to be sensitive to your audience. If you feel that this patter is too morbid for your audience, you can substitute a brighter topic. For example, ask seven volunteers to write true statements about themselves, and one volunteer to write an untrue statement.

If the volunteers' handwriting is illegible, I have them read the cards after I inspect them. This adds to the drama and provides additional misdirection.

Background

Lou Holtz, a legendary football coach at the University of Notre Dame, used this trick to motivate his team; he tore a newspaper and magically restored it (accompanied by inspirational patter). Performing this trick with a paper napkin accomplishes the same principle on a smaller scale.

The Magical Effect

You tear a paper napkin into pieces, explaining that one's life can be torn apart with problems. You explain that those who persevere will emerge strong and whole, and show that the torn napkin has been magically restored into one piece.

Applying the Magic to Presenting and Training

I use this trick to begin or end a workshop on motivation. Each tear of the napkin is a metaphor for life's little pitfalls. I encourage people to keep getting back up because they will eventually be successful. Both adults and children respond to this trick well. The patter can be suited to any situation requiring perseverance through difficulties. I reinforce the theme by reciting the poem *Today*, which I include below.

Materials

- 2 paper napkins (must be exactly alike)
- glue
- 1 paper clip

Torn and Restored Napkin

You find, as a rule, those who complain about the way the ball bounces are usually the ones who dropped it.

—*Unknown*

The Trick, Step by Step

Preparing the napkins:

Step 1:

Unfold the napkins and lay one on top of the other. Glue the top-left corners together using a small dab of glue. Let it dry.

Step 2:

Fold the top napkin into a small square, then place a paper clip on it to hold it in place (Fig. 28-1) until you perform the trick.

Performing the trick:

Step 1:

Remove the paper clip from the napkins without letting the audience see you do so. Hold the napkins so that the audience can see the open napkin but not the folded napkin—it should be concealed by your right hand (Fig. 28-2).

Step 2:

Enumerate a series of problems one may face, each time tearing a small piece of the open napkin, crumpling it, and putting it in your right hand. Repeat until all the visible part of the napkin is torn off.

Step 3:

Explain that one can defeat the problems and emerge whole. Meanwhile, inconspicuously switch the torn pieces with the folded napkin and unfold the napkin. The torn pieces should remain concealed in your right hand. After the audience has seen the "restored" napkin, crumple all the pieces together and throw them away.

Sample Patter

"How is everyone today? One of those days, huh? Well, I know how you feel—I have some rough days myself." I take out the napkins and continue, "In fact, I've had a really rough life. I grew up poor in a rich neighborhood. [I tear the napkin.] I didn't pass my college entrance exam, so I had to go to junior college. [I tear the napkin.] But I had some problems there so I transferred to a college I really didn't want to attend. It was the only one I could afford. [I tear the napkin.] Then I took a job after my college graduation. I really didn't like it either, although it paid okay. [I tear the napkin.] Can you relate to this? Then I was laid off. Downsizing, you know. [I tear the napkin.] At least, that's what they told me. My house burned down and I had no insurance. [I tear the napkin.] You know, I've really had a hard life. Just talking about it makes me wonder how I got here today. "By now the napkin is completely torn and the pieces are in my right hand. "Well, the truth is, my life has been just like this napkin. But after each little pitfall in my life's journey, I just keep moving and striving for my goals." I start to unravel the hidden napkin and continue, "I was actually amazed that each problem was not fatal, and it allowed me to continue with my life. As you heard from my introduction, which was quite good because I wrote it [I pause here for some laughter], my life is as complete as this napkin!" As I proclaim this, I show the magically restored napkin.

"So, I would like to encourage you to always be positive, no matter what happens in your life. Remember that if you can find a path in life with no obstacles, it doesn't lead anywhere." I conclude by reciting the following poem:

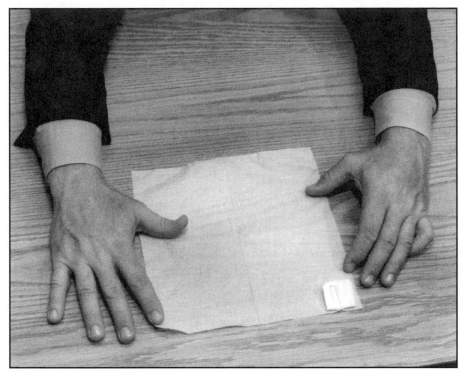

Figure 28-1

Figure 28-2

Today

Each day we live, we never live
again,
But it has a most pronounced effect
on our tomorrows.
As each day passes, we build a
personal history of
Yesterdays which largely chart our
tomorrows.
However, it is the todays in which
things are done.
Yet, like it or not, our use of the
todays is bound
Inseparably to our development of
yesterdays.
So if we are to be masters of our fate
today,

If we are to mold our lives for
contribution today,
If we are to realize the high degree of
personal fulfillment today,
We must deliberately deposit
yesterdays filled with
Honesty, integrity, hard work, and
sincerity—all built
Around unselfish purpose. But today
is the only time
Accounts can be changed. So take
stock and be sure that
The deposits made today will draw
interest in the future.

—*George R. Burns, Ph.D,*
Athens, Georgia

Background

Max Reed of Daytona Beach showed me this trick on a business trip. I made a small change. When he showed me the trick, he said he squeezed the quarter so hard that he made George Washington (whose image is on the quarter) cry. Instead of drawing attention to my strength, I focus on George Washington's self-esteem. When I do this trick I say that harsh words make George Washington cry. I believe that no matter how tough you are, harsh words can hurt your self-esteem. This is an important lesson, especially for leaders.

The Magical Effect

A volunteer says cruel things to the image of George Washington on a quarter and tears flow from the coin.

Applying the Magic to Presenting and Training

I often use this trick to start a discussion about communication and self-esteem. This is a lighthearted way to illustrate the impact of words on self-esteem. This issue is especially important in the workplace. It's extremely important for leaders not to damage their followers' self-esteem with careless words. Maintaining morale is vital to successful leadership.

Materials

- A small ball of wet tissue paper
- A quarter (in case no one in the audience has one)

Please Don't Make George Washington Cry

People ask the difference between a leader and a boss. The leader works in the open, the boss in the covert. The leader leads; the boss drives.
—*Teddy Roosevelt*

The Trick, Step by Step

Step 1:

Conceal the ball of tissue paper in your palm. Borrow a quarter from the audience and place it over the tissue paper (Fig. 29-1). The ball of tissue must be concealed by the coin.

Step 2:

Ask a volunteer to speak harshly to the image of George Washington on the coin. Press on the coin until water drips.

Sample Patter

"Before we start our discussion on effective teamwork, I would like to perform a little demonstration on self-esteem." Borrowing a quarter from the audience, I point out that a picture of George Washington is on the quarter. "Now we all know that this is only a picture of George, but in the world of magic all things are possible. George can hear us. We're here today to discuss how to maintain team members' self-esteem. It's important to understand the power of words. Now, as an example, I want a few people to say some bad things about George." I let several people say bad things about George. When I make the water drip I say, "You see, even George can only take so much before he breaks down. As team members, we need to be aware of how what we say and when we say it can affect our team members."

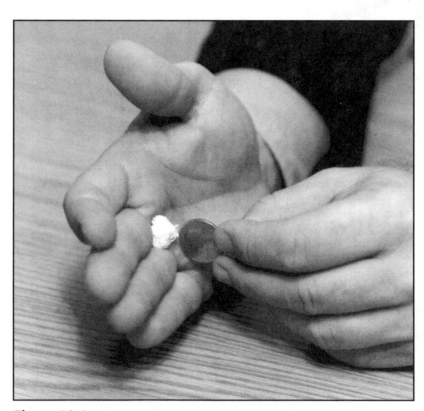

Figure 29-1

Background

While I was preparing for a class one day, Michael Yaffe, my summer intern, approached me with this simple yet provocative exercise. I was impressed with the powerful message of this exercise. It requires people to use real magic: their imaginations.

The Magical Effect

Volunteers are asked to hold a piece of paper with two tears in it (Fig. 30-1) and are challenged to tear it into three pieces without letting go of the corners. Out of your mouth comes an imaginative solution (Fig. 30-2).

Applying the Magic to Presenting and Training

I use this exercise at a class on managing resources. It stimulates creativity and encourages the audience to approach their work with greater imagination. This exercise can be used with a few or hundreds of volunteers, if you provide enough paper. You can have them form teams and address teamwork in problem solving.

Materials

- Several 3" × 5" sheets of paper for each volunteer

The Trick, Step by Step

Step 1:

Make two, equally spaced tears in a paper (Fig. 30-1) and give the paper to a volunteer. Ask the vol-

---

Trick #**30**

Tear and Tear Alike

When you have ruled out all possibilities, it makes the impossible possible.

—*Sherlock Holmes*

Figure 30-1

unteer to tear the paper into three pieces without letting go of the corners. Allow several tries.

Step 2:

Demonstrate the solution: Hold the middle segment with your mouth while tearing (Fig. 30-2).

Sample Patter

At a workshop addressing resource allocation, e.g., goal deployment, I announce, "This exercise will test your most important resource: your creativity. This is an opportunity for you to devise an obvious solution to a not-so-obvious problem." I tell the volunteers that I have plenty of paper, so they may try as many times as they wish.

I make it clear that the only constraint to solving this problem is that one cannot let go of the corners of the paper. After you demonstrate the solution, there will be inevitable complaints from the crowd. I admonish that they need to consider all available resources when undertaking a task. To tear using one's mouth is an innovation, not deception.

Debriefing Questions

- What was your strategy?
- What were your assumptions about this exercise? What tools did you think were available to you?
- Did you benefit from observing or working with others?
- Do you use all the resources available to you at work?
- What resources do you use at work? What resources are available to you?

Figure 30-2

Background

This trick has been around for ages. It's very simple, but when packaged with the right patter, it becomes real magic. You have to perform this trick to fully understand its impact.

The Magical Effect

You pick three cards from a deck and place them on a table. A volunteer takes a random number of cards from the same deck and creates a stack. You divide this new stack into three stacks, turn the top cards over, and they match (card and color) the three cards you originally picked (Fig. 31-1).

Applying the Magic to Presenting and Training

Because the audience needs to see the cards on a table, this trick is not recommended for a large group. I use this card trick to establish good rapport with a small group of people I plan to work with for a while. It works well one-on-one with a client or a student. It's perfect for a business lunch or dinner.

Instead of using a standard deck of cards, you can make your own deck with company products on them or symbols and words appropriate for the occasion.

Materials

- 1 deck of cards

Pick Three

I'm a great believer in luck, and I find the harder I work the more luck I have.

—*Vince Lombardi*

The Trick, Step by Step

Step 1:

Have a volunteer shuffle the deck. Ask the volunteer to pick a number between 3 and 33. While the volunteer is thinking, fan out the cards in your hand, and pick out three cards whose values match the values of the top three cards in the deck. Place them face-up, **left to right,** first putting down the card matching the top card.

Step 2:

Have the volunteer take as many cards from the top of the deck as the number he or she picked, placing them one by one into a stack. The top three cards from the deck become the bottom three cards of this newly created stack, **in reverse order.**

Step 3:

Create three new stacks in front of the three face-up cards by "dealing" from the stack **right to left.** Pay close attention to where the last three cards go. If the number picked by the volunteer is divisible by 3, the last three cards should match the three face-up cards as they are. If not, move the three stacks around to match the face-up cards, remembering that the last three cards dealt out were the first three cards of the original deck, in reverse order.

Step 4:

Reveal the top cards of the three stacks and show that their values match the values of the face-up cards.

Sample Patter

After I have a volunteer shuffle the deck, I ask the volunteer to carefully choose a number between 3 and 33. I continue, "While you're doing that, I'm going to select three cards from the deck at random. Well, almost at random … no, in fact, I'm going to select the ones I want." After I've selected the three cards and laid them face up on the table, I have the volunteer create a new stack by taking as many cards from the top of the deck as the number chosen. Then I say, "Some of you may be wondering what I'm trying to do here. Well, I'm not sure yet, but so far I haven't made any mistakes, have I? Well, if we're on the same wavelength today, it should make our work easier. Not only that, after I divide this stack into three stacks, the top cards should match the values of the cards I picked in the beginning. Wouldn't that be great? Don't get too excited; it doesn't happen very often."

While making the three final stacks, I misdirect their attention by joking, "This is just like Las Vegas. No, forget that. I'm never lucky at those tables." If the stacks need to be switched (because the number chosen by the volunteer is not divisible by 3), I may say, "No, that doesn't feel right. I think I need to make a correction …." Once the three stacks are positioned correctly I have the volunteer turn over the top cards of the three stacks, and I exclaim, "They match! That's amazing. This is only the second time this worked. What do you think this means? I think our minds are on the same wavelength."

Figure 31-1

Background

This is magic for the human soul and spirit. It's an inspirational story that I adapted to promote quality in the workplace. I've used it successfully around the world in training classes and it has been published in numerous company papers around the country. I recommend that you use it like a magic trick; tell the story as if it were your own and adapt it as necessary.

The Magical Effect

A cute, fuzzy doll draws the audience's attention while you entertain and inspire the audience by telling a personal and endearing story.

Applying the Magic to Presenting and Training

Use the story to establish a warm rapport with the audience; let them see you beyond your professional identity. Beginning a presentation by introducing a teddy bear (or a similar doll) has a calming effect. The story can be adapted to many work-related issues.

Materials

1 cute and fuzzy doll

The Trick, Step by Step

Step 1:

Hold the doll and tell the story I give in the sample patter below.

Trick #**32**

The Teddy Bear Story

Even a broken watch is correct twice a day.
—*Unknown*

Sample Patter

The following story actually happened to me with a troll doll, not a teddy bear. As with all magic, however, I freely modified the patter to make the magic flow.

This is my buddy, Mr. William. Let me tell you how we became great partners. It was a typical Saturday morning around my house. I had just gotten up and started getting my things together for a trip to California. In walked my grandson, Justin, who started with the questions.

"Grandpa, where are you going?"

"California."

"Why?"

"For work."

"How long?"

"For a week."

"How long is that?"

"Five days."

"Is Grandma going with you?"

"No."

"Why not?"

"She has to work."

"Why?"

"So we can afford to pay the rent," I joked. He didn't understand the humor and I could see the next question bubbling up in his face. "Won't you be lonely without Grandma?" "Yes, I will." His face immediately showed concern beyond his years. He then ran out of the room and returned shortly holding a brightly-colored little teddy bear. He said, "Grandpa, here, take Mr. William and he will keep you company." I thought for a minute and said, "Sure, that will be great." He smiled to think that now Grandpa would have a friend, and left the room to tell Grandma what he had done. I put the little doll on the bed and finished packing my bags.

After lunch I was ready to leave for the airport, and guess who was coming with me to the airport? Little Justin. We all got into the car and headed to the airport. I checked my bags and started saying my good-byes. As I turned to Justin, I saw him holding the teddy bear. He said, "Grandpa, you almost forgot Mr. William." "Gee, Justin, thanks," I said.

Now, picture this: a 48-year-old man walking through the airport with his teddy bear. Very bright and colorful. I know everybody was looking at me.

I finally got to my seat on the plane and sat down holding the teddy bear. My attention was immediately drawn to the gentleman sitting in the next

Figure 32-1

seat. He appeared very sad. I started a conversation and quickly learned that his wife had died recently and he was going to visit his grandchildren. I shared with him why I was carrying the teddy bear. Without hesitation I asked if he wanted to hold the teddy bear. He laughed. I handed it to him and he took it and smiled. Although he felt a little silly at first, his sadness seemed to subside and he was in better spirits during the flight.

Later on the same flight I heard a little boy a few rows behind me complaining loudly. I was upset by the way the mother was responding to the boy; it seemed a little cruel. I felt especially upset because the boy was Justin's age. I decided to see if I could help. I got up and walked to his seat and asked the mother if there was anything I could do to help. She said no, he was just scared. I went back to my seat and asked the man holding Mr. William if I could borrow him. He smiled as if he knew what I was going to do. I asked the little boy if he would keep Mr. William compa-

ny, because it was Mr. William's first flight and Mr. William was lonely and scared. He said softly, yes, and a slight smile came to his face. The little boy was quiet the rest of the flight!

The boy returned the teddy bear as he got off the plane and instructed me to take good care of Mr. William. I reflected on my trip and realized that I had brought a lot of happiness into those two people's lives with my teddy bear. It's such a simple thing, but so powerful. It was then that I realized that it's the small things we do that make a difference. Little things make a difference at work too. I started looking for small ways to improve the quality of my work.

After I tell the story, people often ask me if the story is true. I could tell them the truth, but that might ruin the magic. Instead I respond with a question—"What do *you* think?"—and smile and continue with the presentation. Alternatively, I might answer that most of it is true and quickly move on.

Background

This trick uses one of the earliest magic props I ever bought, and I still use it wherever I go. When someone says, "So you're a magician; show me a trick," I do this trick and after I'm done, they're convinced I am a magician! This trick can be performed in just a few minutes, although it requires some practice. I have learned how to make the prop and explain it below.

The Magical Effect

You take a dollar bill from the audience and fold it with another dollar bill you are holding, and when you unfold again, the two one-dollar bills have become one two-dollar bill.

Applying the Magic to Presenting and Training

I use this in classrooms, usually when the students are coming back from a break. I've learned that magic focuses students' attention, especially after a break. The trick can symbolize teamwork and synergy. With good patter it should fit into any presentation. You can carry this trick with you always and perform it at meals and meetings. Keep in mind that this trick works best for smaller audiences; everyone needs to be able to see the bills.

Materials

- 1 one-dollar bill
- 1 two-dollar bill

One-Dollar Trick

I am only one, but I am one. I cannot do everything, but I can do something. What I can do, I ought to do, and what I ought to do, by the grace of God I will do.

—*Canon Farrar*

117

- Rubber cement (rubber cement should peel off the bills so that the bills are usable after the trick)

Crisps bills are preferred.

The Trick, Step by Step

Preparing the bills:

Step 1:

Fold both bills as shown in Figures 33-1 through 33-3. Make sharp folds. Unfold the one-dollar bill.

Step 2:

Glue the two-dollar bill (folded) to the lower-right corner of the back side of the one-dollar bill (unfolded) as shown in Figure 33-4. Make sure the corners of the bills match precisely.

Performing the trick:

Step 1:

Show the face of your one-dollar bill to the audience, holding it as shown in Figure 33-5, then show the back side of the bill, concealing the folded two-dollar bill with your right hand as shown in Figure 33-6.

Step 2:

Hold your one-dollar bill with your right hand, showing its face. Borrow a one-dollar bill from the audience, and place it on the outside of your one-dollar bill. Fold the two one-dollar bills together as you did when preparing your bills (Fig. 33-1 to 33-2), except in the last step fold the top half down instead of folding the bottom half up. The folded two-dollar bill has not been shown to the audience yet.

Step 3:

Establish eye-contact with the audience, and flip the folded bills over so that the folded two-dollar bill is showing. Immediately unfold the two-dollar bill and show it to the audience, holding it as shown in Figures 33-5 and 33-6 to conceal the folded one-dollar bills.

Step 4:

Refold the two-dollar bill, flip, then unfold the one-dollar bills, and return the one-dollar bill to the audience.

Position yourself for this trick so that nobody can see from behind you. Practice holding the bills and folding them in front of a mirror until the movements become natural.

Sample Patter

I begin by showing both sides of my one-dollar bill, explaining, "As you can see, I have a garden variety bill with George Washington's picture." When I need to distract their attention so that I can flip over the folded bills, I ask, "When you put two dollar bills together what do you get?" Making eye-contact with the audience is essential to draw their attention away from the folded bills for a moment. Folding the two-dollar bill I continue, "That's right, a two-dollar bill! Thank you. I can see your parents' money was not wasted on your education." After I transform the two-dollar bill back to two one-dollar bills, I hand back the borrowed dollar bill and quickly put away my bills.

Figure 33-1

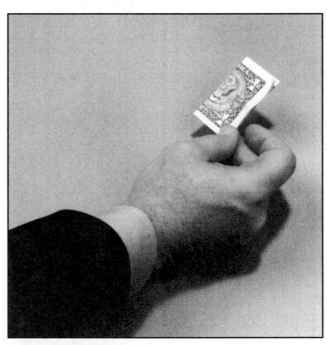

Figure 33-2

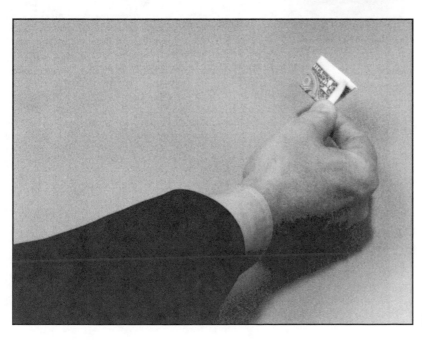

Figure 33-3

Figure 33-4

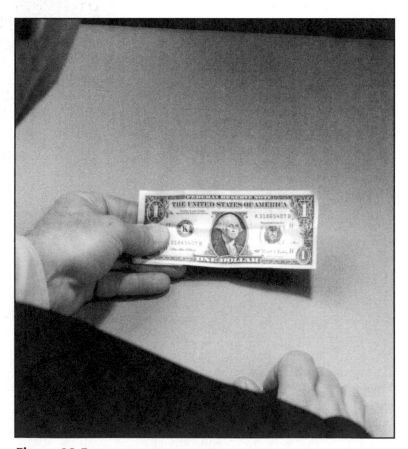

Figure 33-5

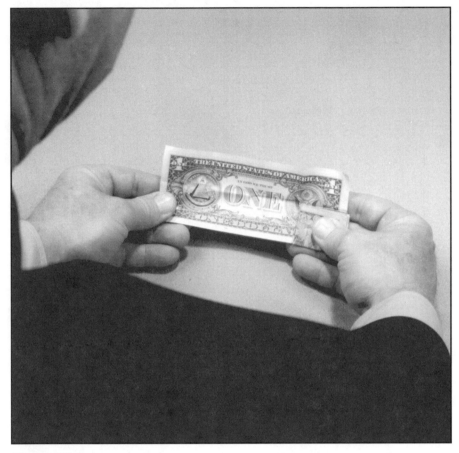

Figure 33-6

Background

Rick Manion, a good friend and an associate, showed me this trick. It has incredible effect but a ridiculously simple secret.

The Magical Effect

A shuffled deck is placed in its case, and you identify each card before you pull it out of the box.

Applying the Magic to Presenting and Training

I use this trick to teach that what you perceive may not be what is actually happening. I also use it to show that effective systems don't have to be complex; I reveal the secret of the trick to the audience after performing the trick and begin a discussion. With silly patter and good acting the trick gets a lot of laughs; it energizes the audience.

Materials

- 1 deck of cards and the case (box)

The Trick, Step by Step

Step 1:

Before the performance, cut a small hole in the case so that you can read the card inside (Fig. 34-1).

Step 2:

Ask a volunteer to shuffle a deck of cards. Take the shuffled deck and put it inside the case so that you can read the bottom card through the hole.

Trick #34

The Incredible Card Reader

You cannot discover new oceans unless you have the courage to lose sight of the shore.
—Unknown

Step 3:

Glance through the hole to identify the bottom card, announce the value of the card, then pull it out of the case and show it to the audience. Repeat several times.

Sample Patter

"I didn't get any sleep last night preparing this trick. I hope you don't get any sleep while I'm doing this trick!" I ask a volunteer to thoroughly shuffle the deck. Before I place the shuffled deck in the case, I ask, "Is there any way I could know the order of the cards after you shuffled them? No. I have, however, completed the world's best class in memory improvement." I thumb through the deck quickly—so quickly that it's impossible to see the faces of the cards—and pretend that I am memorizing the cards. After putting the cards into the case I announce, "I will try to remember the order of the cards." I announce the value of a card, pull it out of the box and show it to the audience. After identifying many cards I conclude, "You see, hard work and long hours do pay off. My memory is incredible!"

Figure 34-1

Background

This is really a spin-off of Trick #33, One-Dollar Trick. Instead of transforming two $1 bills into one $2 bill, you transform a $1 bill into a $100 bill.

The Magical Effect

A $1 bill is transformed into a $100 bill in your hands. That's an amazing ROI (return on investment)!

Applying the Magic to Presenting and Training

Transforming a $1 bill into a $100 bill should grab the attention of anyone in business. I use this trick while playing a business simulation game called *Zodiak: The Game of Business Finance and Strategy* (Paradigm Learning, Inc., Tampa, FL). *Zodiak* is a basic but powerful game that allows employees to experience the impact of business decisions. Transforming a $1 bill into a $100 bill focuses their attention on ROI. I've also used this magic trick to convince our salespeople that our product will increase our customers' ROI; it encourages our salespeople to be more persuasive. You can use this trick in a presentation about teamwork: Each fold of the $1 bill is a contribution by a team member, and the result is much greater than the sum of individual contributions.

Materials

- 1 $1 bill
- 1 $100 bill

Trick **#35**

Return on Investment (ROI)

Today's trying times will have become 'the good old days' in twenty years.

—*Unknown*

125

- Rubber cement (rubber cement should peel off the bills so that the bills are usable after the trick)

The Trick, Step by Step

Step 1:

Fold and glue the bills together as described in Trick #33.

Step 2:

Conduct the trick as described in Trick #33, except without laying a borrowed $1 bill on top of your bills.

Sample Patter

After we play a round of *Zodiak* I perform this magic trick. "Can everyone see what I have in my hand? Yes, it's a $1 bill. This is what business is all about—taking a dollar and making more, right? For example, if I take this dollar and invest it, what should I expect to get in return? Yes, profit! The more the better." I fold the $1 bill while I talk: I tell the audience that every fold of this dollar represents an investment decision. "I've made several investment decisions for my dollar. I should expect a good ROI. What do you think that should be? How do my decisions affect ROI?" After briefly discussing some of the answers, I unfold the $1 bill and reveal that my investment has transformed the $1 bill into $100. I marvel that that is an astonishing ROI: 10,000%! "So, in the next round of *Zodiak*, you'll make business decisions for yourselves and see how that affects your ROI."

Background

A professional comedian seems to know just the right thing to say at just the right time. I once asked Frankie Paul, a professional comedian, how he was able to accomplish this feat. He replied, "It's a matter of practice. I memorize various catch-phrases and practice them. When it's time to use them, they just seem to come out." A good presenter should be able to say just the right thing at just the right time too; humor enlivens your presentation. I believe that all presenters should build a repertoire of one-liners and anecdotes and practice them. I will share with you the ones I've collected and used. Many of them come from Harry Allen, a famous magician who now lives in Daytona Beach, Florida, and runs a magic store. His book, *A Sleight of Mouth,* is available in many magic shops.

The Magical Effect

Have you ever been in a situation when you wished you had something clever to say? If you learn these one-liners and anecdotes, you will.

Applying the Magic to Presenting and Training

Stories and one-liners are good for the beginning of presentations. I also use the one-liners to add a little humor when I make a mistake while performing a magic trick. You'll find many occasions for one-liners during your presentation.

Materials

- None

Trick #**36**

One-Liners and Anecdotes

There is a big difference between free speech and cheap talk.

—*Unknown*

The Trick, Step by Step

Step 1:

The secret to this magic trick is practice! Practice these one-liners with family and friends. Also, it is important that the one-liners and anecdotes fit your personality. Be careful about making fun of anyone in the audience. The best person to ridicule is yourself or a co-presenter.

One-Liners for Opening Your Presentation

- Good evening, my name is Ed Rose, and of course you should all know yours!
- Before I speak, I have something very important to say. (*Groucho Marx*)
- Well, I hope you've enjoyed yourselves up until now because this is where we separate the real listeners from the steady, fixed stares.
- Please raise your hand in the back of the room if you can't hear my voice! (Pause.) Some of the people in the front of the room may want to come back there and join you.

One-Liners after a Good Introduction

- Isn't it amazing what people will say when they aren't under oath?
- That was a great introduction—I know, I wrote it.
- I really wanted to get here in the worst way. I took the interstate. Believe me, that was the worst way!
- After that introduction I want more money, any money.
- How do you like the clothes? I'm thinking about buying them.
- I come from a very large family. You may know them: mammals!
- Hi, my name is Ed Rose. If that alone isn't enough, I'll do my presentation.
- [Walk into the room and take a drink. Don't say anything for a minute. Then say:] What's wrong? When you got your job did you start right away?
- There is no excuse for the way I'm about to behave.

One-Liners for Card Tricks

- [When you hand someone the deck, say:] Shuffle the cards but don't mix them. That will make the trick a lot harder.
- Please examine the deck. A stacked deck may mean nothing to you, but it means a great deal to my next trick.
- Please pick a card and show it to your friends—I'm sure that won't take long.
- First, before you think of a card, empty your mind. That won't take but seconds.
- Pick a card. Thanks. Now, do you want to change your mind, or are you happy with the one you have?
- Do you know one card from another? Yes? That's too bad! I'll have to use someone else.
- [If you select the wrong card, turn the card over and say:] Well, at least the backs match.
- Trust everybody, but always cut the cards.

One-Liner All-Purpose Fillers

- What do you give somebody that has everything? Penicillin.

- We now have 35 million laws trying to enforce ten commandments.

- I've never been poor, only broke. The difference is that poor is a state of mind, while being broke is only a temporary situation.

- When I was six years old my family moved. Don't worry, I found them again!

- What time is it? Three o'clock? You know, I've asked that question three times today and I keep getting different answers.

- The thing I like best about egotists is that they don't go around talking about other people.

- Do you want to feel younger? Hang around old people.

One-Liners to Handle Disruptions to Your Presentation

- [When a small group of people are talking, say:] I see we've started to break up in little discussion groups.

- [When you mispronounce a word, say:] First day with a new mouth.

- [When you mispronounce a word, say:] Isn't that how it works? You pay $2,000 for new lips and now the tongue doesn't work.

- [When there is a lot of noise coming from an adjacent room, say:] Sounds like my kids are studying next door.

- [When someone points out a spelling mistake, say:] Wasn't it

W.C. Fields who said "Never trust a person who can only spell a word one way"? Well, you know you can trust me.

- [When someone points out a spelling mistake, say:] That's right, go ahead and laugh. The spell checker on my computer laughs at me too!

- [When someone drops something on the floor, say:] That's fine; just put it anywhere.

- [When a beeper goes off, say:] Beam me up, Scottie!

- [When an ambulance siren is heard, say:] Well, I'll be leaving now. My ride is here. [Take a step toward the door.]

Motivational Quotations and Proverbs

- It's easy to get good players. Gettin' 'em to play together, that's the hard part. (*Casey Stengel*)

- Don't ever slam the door. Some day you might want to go back in. (*Irish proverb*)

- Problems are opportunities in work clothes.

- You can't escape the responsibility of tomorrow by evading it today. (*Abraham Lincoln*)

- If coaching is everything, why can't a coach teach a sub to play as well as the best player? (*Abe Lemons*)

- You don't learn anything when you win, but when you lose, you'd better learn!

- Don't hesitate to ask dumb questions—they're easier to handle than dumb mistakes.

- People are like teabags—you never know how strong they'll be until they're in hot water. (*Rita Mae Brown*)

- Advice is what we ask for when we know the answer but wish we didn't. (*Erica Jong*)

- You've got to do your own growing, no matter how tall your grandfather was. (*Irish Proverb*)

- A conclusion is a place where you get tired of thinking. (*Fischer's Law*)

- Progress is a nice word, but change is its motivator, and change has enemies. (*Robert F. Kennedy*)

- The good thing about being young is that you are not experienced enough to know you cannot possibly do the things you are doing.

- A good team reacts; a great team anticipates.

- Remember—it wasn't raining when Noah started building the ark. (*Howard Ruff*)

- You can't tell which way the train went by looking at the tracks.

An Anecdote to Motivate Teamwork

A magician was practicing his magic and needed some quiet time to fine-tune his newest illusion. His ten-year-old son came into the room wanting to play with him. Not wanting to hurt his son's feelings, he thought of a good way to keep him occupied for a long time. He took a map of the world and ripped it into one hundred small pieces. He gave it to his son and sent him into the next room, telling him that when he finished putting the world back together, they would play together. Off went the boy, and the magician thought he had hours to practice his magic. In five minutes the boy returned and told his father that he had completed the puzzle. In disbelief, the father followed his son into the next room to see for himself. Sure enough, the puzzle pieces were put together correctly. "How did you get it together so fast?" asked the father. "It was easy," said the son, smiling, as he turned over the map of the world. "You see, Dad, on the other side of the map are pictures of people, and when you put the people together, the world comes together!" If the members of a team rally around a common goal, individual differences can be overcome.

Background

This is a vintage case of "magician force," where a seemingly random choice is actually forced by the magician. There is no exotic illusion but there is an eye-catching effect. Because the trick can be obvious to many, I often do this one tongue-in-cheek rather than trying to be a David Copperfield. The trick is simple, so it's easy to perform too!

The Magical Effect

A large card randomly selected out of five cards by a volunteer has today's presentation topic written on it.

Applying the Magic to Presenting and Training

You can open any presentation using this trick.

Materials

- 5 large cards. Four of them should have irrelevant topics written on them. One of them should have today's presentation topic written on it.

The Trick, Step by Step

Step 1:
Give the cards to five volunteers and have them stand in front of the audience. Remember which volunteer is holding the card with today's topic written on it. Ask the five volunteers to hold the cards in front of them but not reveal the writing on them to anyone.

Trick #37

Point to a Topic

Do not fear the winds of adversity—remember a kite rises against the wind rather than with it.
—*Unknown*

131

Step 2:

Find a sixth volunteer. Ask this volunteer to point to three of the five cards. If the card with today's topic is selected, ask the two unselected volunteers to put their cards down and return to their seats. If the card with today's topic is not selected, ask the selected volunteers to put their cards down and return to their seats.

Step 3:

If there are three cards remaining, ask the sixth volunteer to point to two of the three cards. If there are two cards remaining, ask the sixth volunteer to point to one of the two cards. In both cases, if the card with today's topic is selected, ask the volunteer(s) holding the unselected card(s) to sit; if the card with today's topic is not selected, as the volunteer(s) holding the selected card(s) to sit.

Step 4:

Reveal the four unselected cards, then ask the remaining volunteer to show the card to the audience.

Note: When asking the sixth volunteer to select cards, use the word "point." It misdirects the audience better than other words. I have found that using the words "select" or "choose" often tips off the audience to the secret of the trick. Also, guiding the sixth volunteer quickly through the choices (the pointing) is helpful in preventing the audience from thinking about the trick.

Sample Patter

I may begin a presentation of leadership like this: "I'd like to let you choose what I'm going to talk about today. I know you're all expecting a presentation on leadership and I did prepare for that subject. I have four other topics, however, that may also be fun to talk about."

I have the five cards in a stack facing down on a table. The fourth card from the top has leadership written on it. The other cards have weather, sports, politics, and animals written on them. I give out the cards one at a time to five volunteers. This makes it easy to remember which volunteer gets the card with leadership on it. To distract the audience a little, I say to the volunteers, "Hold the cards in front of you but please do not show the writing to the audience or look at it yourselves. I wouldn't want you to give eye signals to anyone."

To select the sixth volunteer I joke, "Now I need someone who can make decisions and can point. Do we have any managers in the room?" After the volunteer points to three cards, I quip, "That was a real quick decision; you may have a great future ahead of you in some kind of management position. In fact, if my magic doesn't work tonight, you may get a chance at some public speaking."

Before I reveal the one remaining card, I reveal the four discarded cards. "Let's look at what we could have been talking about tonight. I'm having so much fun, I'm almost too nervous to look! We could have talked about the weather. We could have talked about sports. You don't want to talk about politics. And you don't want to talk about animals." After I reveal the card with leadership on it, I add a little misdirection by reminding the audience that the volunteer freely chose the card.

Trick #38

The Easiest Mind-Reading Trick in the World

Many new ideas are simply clever adaptations of old ideas.

—*Thomas Edison*

Background

The idea for this trick came from the world-famous magician and master of ceremonies, Karrell Fox. The secret of this trick is so simple you will be flabbergasted. When done right, though, it looks like real mind reading.

The Magical Effect

You select a volunteer from a large audience, and correctly guess the volunteer's name.

Applying the Magic to Presenting and Training

This trick works well as an icebreaker with a large audience. Obviously, you can't use it when everyone's name is known (e.g., when everyone is wearing name tags).

Materials

- None

The Trick, Step by Step

Step 1:
  Loudly select a volunteer from the audience and have the volunteer come up to the front of the room.

Step 2:
  Quietly ask the volunteer for his or her name, so that the audience does not hear you or the volunteer.

Step 3:
  Loudly announce to the audience that you will guess the volunteer's name. Loudly ask the volunteer to

think of his or her name. Contort your body as if you are mind reading, then loudly announce the name.

Note: If there is a microphone, speak into it for Steps 1 and 3 and step away from it for Step 2. If you are wearing a microphone, turn if off or cover it inconspicuously for Step 2.

Sample Patter

"Before I start tonight, I'd like to do a little something special. Let me go into the audience and get a victim, I mean, helper." I try to avoid the loud, outspoken type—if it is possible to tell—and try to select someone who seems quiet. After leading the volunteer up to the front of the room and after I've learned the volunteer's name, I say loudly, "Well, thank you for volunteering to help me. Have we ever met before? Did I call you before today to set up a trick? I'd like you to silently think of your name and concentrate while I try to read your mind." I briefly make faces and contort my body to act as if I'm reading the volunteer's mind. Finally I shout the volunteer's name, then turn to the volunteer and ask, "Is that indeed your name?"

Background

This trick has been used by amateur and professional magicians around the world.

The Magical Effect

You burn a dollar bill after having a volunteer write down its serial number. You then point to an envelope attached to the bottom of a chair, and inside is a dollar bill with the same serial number. The bill wasn't burned after all!

Applying the Magic to Presenting and Training

This trick is useful for broaching a discussion on how people's perceptions of the same event are different. It also works well for amusing business clients at a dinner meeting. Performing the trick in a small group requires more agility and practice than doing it for large groups.

Materials

- 2 new dollar bills with serial numbers in sequential order (banks often give out uncirculated bills in sequential order)
- 1 ordinary pencil eraser
- 1 envelope and some tape
- 1 lighter and 1 ashtray
- 1 large piece of paper and 1 pen

The Trick, Step by Step

Step 1:

Erase the last digit of the serial numbers of the dollar bills. This makes the remaining serial num-

Trick #**39**

Money to Burn

Any fool can criticize, condemn and complain—and most do.

—*Dale Carnegie*

bers identical. Wrinkle both bills (it makes it more difficult to see that numbers have been erased) and put one of them into an envelope. Seal the envelope and tape it under a chair in the front row of the room. Conceal the other dollar bill in your sleeve.

Step 2:

Have a volunteer come to the front of the room. Ask for another volunteer to give you a dollar. Choose one in the back of the room, and walk to the volunteer to receive the dollar bill. As you return to the front of the room, switch the dollar bill you received with the one you concealed in your sleeve.

Step 3:

Ask the volunteer to write the serial number of the dollar bill on a large piece of paper, then burn the bill in an ashtray.

Step 4:

Ask the person sitting on the chair with the envelope taped to it to find it and bring it to you. Have the person open the envelope, read the bill and confirm that it matches the serial number written on the paper.

Note: If you are unable to switch the bills while returning from the back of the room, you can ask the volunteer to write his or her name on a piece of paper and take that moment to make the switch.

Sample Patter

When I give my switched bill to the volunteer, I ask, "Is this is an ordinary dollar bill, or did you just make it?" After the bill's serial number is written down I place the paper where everyone can see it. I like to ask the volunteer to burn the bill by saying, "Now, would you please light the bill?" and handing the volunteer a flashlight. (Wait for laughter.) After I have the volunteer burn the dollar bill, I ask the audience if they believe that the bill was really burned. I ask those who believe that it was not burned to raise their hands. Often some will raise their hands and I ask them, "If the bill didn't burn, what do you think happened?" I note aloud that we observed the same event but have different perceptions of what happened.

Before I reveal the hidden bill I explain, "What we're going to work on today is the need to probe for the facts in problem solving, because what you see may not be what actually happened. For example, a large percentage of you believe the dollar bill was burned, and in reality it was just an illusion." I then ask the person sitting on the chair with the envelope taped to it to look for it and bring it to me. "Please open the envelope and read the serial number. Is the number the same as the serial number written down previously? You see, the bill was not actually burned. I created the illusion of actually burning it."

Debriefing Questions

- How many, by a show of hands, believe me?
- How many are not sure what to believe?
- What do you need to make a better decision on whether the bill was burned or not?

Background

I learned the basis for the trick from a good friend, John Emerson, on a business trip. It starts out like a magic trick but is actually a joke. It makes me laugh and I love it. I apply the Magic Principles to shape the delivery of the joke for each presentation, and have found that audiences love it.

The Magical Effect

You write something on a piece of paper and fold it. Then a volunteer is asked to pick a number between 1 and 100, and everyone thinks you predicted the number and wrote it on the paper. When you show the paper, however, it only has a funny punch line written on it.

Applying the Magic to Presenting and Training

This is only a spoof of magic, but often it's just what the doctor ordered. You can use it to lighten up the atmosphere with any size audience. You can use it at a dinner meeting to break the ice and establish a friendly rapport; it shows that you don't take yourself too seriously. I sometimes use it to discuss effective communication. When one side gives directions and the other side is not allowed to ask questions, the results can be unexpected (as in this trick).

Materials

- A large piece of paper and a pen

Trick #40

That's Right

It's good to have a train of thought provided you have a terminal.

—*Unknown*

The Trick, Step by Step

Step 1:

Ask for everyone's attention. Act as if you are concentrating, then write "That's right" on a piece of paper without letting the audience see it. Fold the paper and place it in a conspicuous place.

Step 2:

Ask a volunteer to think of a number between 1 and 100. Ask the volunteer if he or she wants to change the number. Then ask the volunteer, "Do you correctly remember the number?" When the volunteer answers yes, have them articulate the number. Ask the volunteer to unfold the paper and show it to the audience. Everyone expects to see a number but instead sees "That's right" and laughs.

Sample Patter

I set up the joke by announcing, "I'm going to do something that will amaze and confuse you." Once I have a volunteer pick a number, I pester him or her by saying, "Do you really have the number in your head? Would you like to change your mind? No? So you're happy with the one you have?" Before I get to the punch line, I prepare the audience one more time; I want them to think that I'm performing a typical magic trick. I say, "Okay, here is the amazing moment! Are you ready?" Then I ask the volunteer, "Do you know the number you selected?" Once the volunteer says yes, I ask them to share the number with the group. I hand the volunteer the folded paper and ask him or her to show it to the rest of the group. I conclude by saying, "It's important that you understand my presentation clearly, so please feel free to ask questions during my presentation."

Debriefing Questions

- What were you expecting?
- Did I mislead you? Did you mislead yourself?
- Does this type of communication ever happen where you work?
- How could you understand better what I was doing?

Background

I was inspired by a comedy act to create this trick. The subliminal suggestions don't always work, but it's a surefire crowd pleaser.

The Magical Effect

A volunteer is challenged to guess the word you wrote on a piece of paper. Prompted by your subliminal suggestions, the volunteer indeed guesses the word you wrote.

Applying the Magic to Presenting and Training

This is a fun icebreaker for large and small groups. I do this trick at dinner meetings using paper napkins. I also use it to promote effective sales presentations.

Materials

- A large piece of paper and a pen

The Trick, Step by Step

Step 1:

Ask a volunteer to come stand in front of you. Try to pick someone who would not deliberately try to spoil the trick. Write the word "No" on a piece of paper without letting anyone see the word, then fold the paper.

Step 2:

Ask the volunteer to guess the word you wrote. Reiterate your request several times using the words "no" and "know," subtly accentuating these words when you speak.

Subliminal Suggestions

Why do we do what we do, when we know what we know?
—Denis Waitley

Step 3:

After the volunteer gives an answer, reveal the word you wrote on paper.

There are alternative subliminal suggestion tricks you can use. Explain to the audience that you would like to go over some facts, then ask a question.

- Have the audience say and spell "silk." Repeat several times, then ask, "What do cows drink?" Most will say milk instead of water.

- Have the audience say and spell "pots." Repeat several times, then ask, "What do you do when you come to a green light?" Most will say "stop" instead of "go."

Sample Patter

In order to get the volunteer to say "no" I use the following subliminal suggestions: "Did you *know* you would be doing this today?" "*No* one is to help you out; you must do this on your own." "There is to be absolutely *no* wild guessing." "Do you *know* what the word is?" "You should *know* the word by simply concentrating."

Background

The idea for this trick came to me at the 1996 International Brotherhood of Magicians' Conference in Norfolk, Virginia. After that I read David Harkey's *Found in Bermuda* and was inspired by it to develop the idea further. In this book, Harkey uses tiny model airplanes to perform a trick similar to mine. I discussed this trick with my colleague Mike Yaffe for weeks before we discovered a form that works in our presentations.

The Magical Effect

A total of 27 game pieces are laid out on a table to form a triangle in such a way that on each side there are 13 pieces. New pieces are added to the triangle and some are shifted around. Volunteers are asked to take inventory of the triangle after each addition. Magically, the number of pieces on all sides remains equal.

Applying the Magic to Presenting and Training

This is a fun way to illustrate systematic problems in an organization. It adapts well to any type of organization: Just use the organization's products as game pieces. For example, when I do this trick for a semiconductor manufacturer, I use computer chips as game pieces. In a pinch, no special props are needed; pennies work just fine. Sometimes pennies are quite appropriate. I've seen this trick used to illustrate a money-laundering scheme, where the observers lose track of money added to the trian-

Trick #42

Stuck on 13

Education is the ability to listen to almost anything without losing your temper or your self-confidence.

—*Robert Frost*

gle. The trick works well for both small and large audiences. If you have a large audience, be sure to use large game pieces so that everyone can see them.

Materials

- 32 game pieces
- A table

The Trick, Step by Step

Step 1:

Lay 27 game pieces on a table in the way shown in Figure 42-1. Each corner has four pieces, and each side consists of two clusters, a two-piece cluster and a three-piece cluster.

Step 2:

Designate three volunteers as managers. Tell them that each

one is responsible for one side of the triangle.

Step 3:

Give a new game piece to one of the managers, with instructions to add it to any of the clusters on his or her side of the triangle. If the manager adds it to a corner, move a piece from each of the other two corners into the opposite side (Fig. 42-2). If the manager adds the new piece to a side, move a corner piece from that side to an adjacent side (Fig. 42-3).

Step 4:

Take a side piece and add it to a second side; then take a piece from the second side and add it to the third side; then take a piece from the third side and add it to the first side (Fig. 42-4). This step moves pieces in a circular pattern and does not affect the count on each side. It is for misdirection.

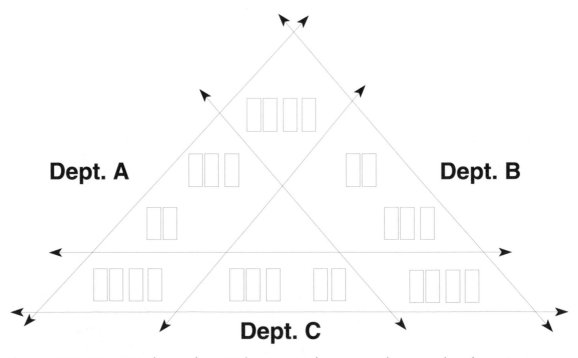

Figure 42-1. Fig. 42-1 shows the initial setup. Make sure each corner has four pieces, with two- and three-piece units alternating on either side.

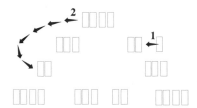

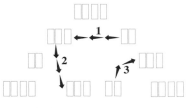

Figure 42-2. Fig. 42-2 shows how to react to a piece that has been added to one of the corners. Simply slide a piece from each of the other corners to the row facing the corner where the piece was added.

Figure 42-3. Fig. 42-3 shows how one might react when a piece is added to one of the sides. You only need to move one piece from one of the corners of that side to the middle of the next row.

Figure 42-4. Fig. 42-4 is an example of a series of moves that do not affect the number of parts in each row. Such movements should be combined with those illustrated in Figures 42-2 and 42-3.

Step 5:

Ask the managers to take inventory of their sides of the triangle and report to the audience.

Step 6:

Repeat Steps 3–5 several times.

Note: The key to this trick is that the pieces in the corners are counted twice, once for each side that shares that corner, whereas the pieces on the sides are counted only once. When a new piece is added you react by moving pieces away from the corners (where they are counted twice) to the sides (where they are counted once). The number of new pieces that can be added is limited by the number of pieces that remain in the corners. Do not add more than 4 or 5 pieces, because you may run out of corner pieces to use or because you may get confused yourself and move pieces incorrectly.

Sample Patter

I use this trick often at workshops dealing with communication among departments. "Dr. Edward Deming said, '85 percent of a company's defects are usually systematic.' If workers in an organization can't communicate with one another, that makes it difficult to resolve issues. And when issues are left unresolved, your productivity goes down. When productivity goes down, the organization suffers as a whole. Let me show you what I'm talking about."

When I designate volunteers to be managers of the sides of the triangle, I name the sides of the triangle with appropriate names. For example, I may name one volunteer the manager of the company's New York office, another the manager of the company's Chicago office, and the third the manager of the company's San Francisco office. I ask the managers to stand on the sides of the triangle they are in charge of. I tell them that because they are in different cities they are temporarily out of touch with each other and are not allowed to consult with each other during this exercise.

When I move pieces around in response to the addition of a new piece, I say "Okay, the Chicago office needs a new shipment here, and the San Francisco office requests a transfer of some products here, and this product is defective so it is sent back to the New York Office." After I move the pieces around and the managers report their inventories, I ask the managers if they know what is happening.

Debriefing Questions

- What happened to the company's overall inventory?

- What happened to each department's inventory?

- Did the managers know what was happening?

- What would have happened if the managers closely consulted each other after each addition?

- Do you understand how your department relates to other departments?

- What can improve communication at your workplace?

Background

This is a standard trick for magicians at children's birthday parties. I haven't performed at children's birthday parties in a long time, but I dusted it off and gave it a new twist for an adult audience. I use it to suggest that the audience will add the much-needed color into a class just as the crayons add color to a coloring book. You may thing this trick is too basic—but it will definitely amuse the audience.

The Magical Effect

You open a coloring book and show that the pages are not colored. You close the coloring book and pass a box of crayons behind it. When you open the coloring book, the pages are colored.

The Magic Coloring Book

If it's to be, it's up to me.

—*Unknown*

Applying the Magic to Presenting and Training

You can use this trick to encourage participation; you can tell the audience that participation will add color to the workshop. The colors can be a metaphor for the diverse talents in a team; you can say that for a complete picture to form, all the talents have to cooperate. You may also say that good teamwork is a form of art.

Materials

- 1 magic coloring book from a magic shop
- 1 box of magic crayons from a magic shop

The Trick, Step by Step

Follow the simple instructions included with the magic coloring book.

Sample Patter

I may begin a workshop like this: "This coloring book is just like this class. You come in with no knowledge of the subject today. My job is to provide you with structure—an outline of what we need to learn—but you will be providing the key ingredients to make the picture complete." Picking up the box of crayons, I say, "These crayons symbolize you, the class." As I move the box of crayons behind the coloring book I say, "Just as the crayons put color into the coloring book, you will put the color into today's class."

Background

This trick originates from the famous Paul Diamond, now a retired magician living in Ft. Lauderdale, Florida. I met Paul at the Hank Lee Magic Conference at Cape Cod, where he showed me how to make water disappear from a cup. My innovation is to use this trick to discuss levels of trust between people.

The Magical Effect

You wave your hand over a cup of water and claim that you made it disappear. You go from volunteer to volunteer until you find one who trusts you enough to tilt the cup over his or her head. When you do, nothing comes out!

Trick #44

Levels of Trust

Remember, it's only magic if it's not your trick.
—Ray Green

Applying the Magic to Presenting and Training

This is an excellent way to show that there are different levels of trust. Some people will believe that you made the water disappear but not enough to let you tilt the cup over their heads. I use a chart describing three different levels of trust (Fig. 44-1) to launch a discussion about trust. I tell the audience that the volunteer's willingness to let me tilt the cup over his or her head is an example of "Level 3" of trust—faith—since the volunteer's willingness goes beyond facts.

This trick is also appropriate for presentations regarding teamwork, since trust is an essential ingredient in teamwork.

Materials

- 1 paper or styrofoam cup
- A pitcher of water
- A packet of Slush Powder, also known as Gel Powder. It is inexpensive and available in most magic shops. When water is added, it absorbs all the water and sticks to the cup.

The Trick, Step by Step

Step 1:

Pour water into a cup containing Slush Powder. Tell the audience that you will make the water disappear. Wave your hand over the cup.

Step 2:

Ask people in the audience if they believe that you made the water disappear. Ask those who say yes if you may tilt the cup over their heads. If anyone says yes, tilt the cup over his or her head. If no one says yes, ask the same questions to other people in the audience. Go from person to person until you find someone who will let you tilt the cup over his or her head. If you cannot find anyone, tilt it over in front of you. Don't force anyone to participate. When they see the cup turned over without water coming out, they will get the message.

Note: Be careful not to raise the cup high enough so the audience can look inside the cup.

Sample Patter

I like to preface this trick with a joke: I pour water into a cup and ask, "Does anyone believe I can make this water disappear?" When people shake their heads, I promptly drink the water and smile. For the trick, I pour water from a cup into another one containing Slush Powder. I toss the empty cup for effect. When I ask someone if I may tilt the cup over his or her head, I make an intentional slip, saying, "Do you trust me enough to let me *pour*, I mean tilt, the cup over your head?" This slip helps add suspense to the trick. In addition, being hesitant or making a few aborted attempts to tilt the cup before actually doing so makes the audience wonder if there is water in the cup, adding suspense.

Debriefing Questions

- Why did you trust me to tilt the cup over your head?
- How did you reach that level of trust with me?
- How can you relate this to the concept of establishing trust with others (teams, etc.)?

Figure 44-1

Levels of Trust

Level 1 - TRUSTWORTHINESS:
Building a foundation with Actions

Team members' characteristics and attributes that lead to trust (i.e., integrity, dependability, and openness) and allow them to build trusting relationships with other team members.

Level 2 - CONSISTENCY:
Members can be counted on

Team members have developed collaborative relationships through their trustworthiness. This provides a strong base that insulates the relationship from collapsing under difficult conditions.

Level 3 - FAITH:
Goes beyond facts

Team members experience this level of trust when trust has become an integral part of the relationship. Members freely open up to each other. This level of trust is based on faith. It goes beyond the facts, as in the example of the water disappearing: We all know that no one can make water disappear.

Figure 44-2

Background

This trick uses a common magician's device to symbolize the power of teamwork. I first tested this trick in May, 1996, when I conducted a team-building workshop for 80 European executives. I wanted to create a bond among the people of various European cultures, so I used this trick on the opening night to symbolize the unity that is possible among the participants. It was a great success.

The Magical Effect

Explaining that you want to harness the energy of the audience, you ask everyone in the audience to form a chain by touching another person with his or her right forefinger. You are the last link in the chain, and when you are touched a ball of fire shoots from your hand.

Applying the Magic to Presenting and Training

I mostly use this fiery trick to talk about teamwork, synergy, and motivation; but fire is a great way to grab attention at any kind of a presentation. I've used it to start a seminar with high school students in order to excite them and promote participation.

Materials

- 1 magician's fire-shooting device

There are many types of fire-shooting devices available at magic shops. They vary in power, size, and methods of concealment. Consider your

---

_{Trick} #45

Harnessing Team Energy

Failure is not fatal and success isn't permanent.

—*Don Shula*

151

dress and the locations of your presentations when selecting one. One that I like to use is the *Gem Hand Flasher* by Gem Magic Mfg. (206)778-2076, $10–$15. It's small and fits nicely in one hand (Fig. 45-1). Although these devices are safe when used correctly, they should always be handled with caution. Remember that you are not allowed to hand carry these devices onto a plane. You must pack them in your checked luggage.

several separate chains may form. You may need to direct people so that one long chain is formed.

Step 2:

Position yourself at one end of the chain so that the hand with the fire-shooting device is away from the end. Ask the person at the end of the chain to touch your shoulder. As this person touches you, raise the hand with the device and trigger the device.

The Trick, Step by Step

Step 1:

Announce that you would like to harness the energy in the audience. Ask the audience to form a chain by having each person touch another person with his or her right forefinger. In a crowded room

Sample Patter

At the beginning of a workshop I announce, "I'd like to try to harness the energy in this room." At this point, I begin playing some upbeat background music. "You know that our thoughts and our feelings are forms of energy. Each of us carries

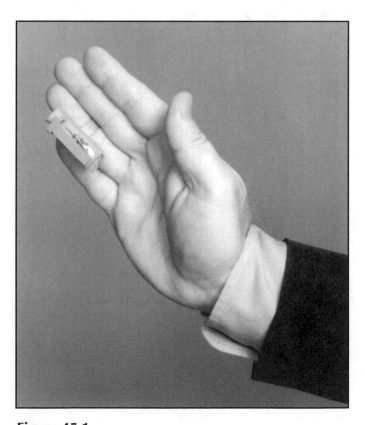

Figure 45-1

with us energy that is our dreams, our inspirations, our heartbeats. It's this energy that comes together when we work in teams. I'd like us to link everyone's personal energy into team energy. Everyone please form a single chain by touching the person next to you with your right forefinger. I will become the last link in the chain, a lightning rod for all our energy." Before I let the person at the end of the chain touch me, I call everyone's attention to my hand. Making sure that I am not pointing the device at a fire sprinkler, I shoot fire. I congratulate and thank the audience by asking them to applaud themselves.

Background

When I first saw this trick I couldn't believe my eyes. It requires absolutely no sleight of hand; the secret is built into the magic kit. You do have to provide an important ingredient, however: good patter to make this trick contribute to your presentation.

The Magical Effect

You blow through a pipe that has a piece of string coming out of it (Fig. 46-1). A bracelet appears to pass right through the string.

Applying the Magic to Presenting and Training

You can use this trick to teach that what seems impossible may be possible. You can use this trick to begin a presentation on motivation or problem solving. The simple yet amazing effect makes it a great attention-grabber for any presentation.

Materials

- 1 *GLO-Loop* by Frank Herman. It costs $5–$10 and is available at most magic shops.
- 1 cheap plastic bracelet

The Trick, Step by Step

Blow into a *GLO-Loop* and slowly pass a bracelet through the string.

Sample Patter

I begin my performance by making sure that everyone can see me well.

Trick #46

The Impossible Is Possible

Things may come to those who wait, but only the things left by those who hustle.

—Abraham Lincoln

Figure 46-1

Before I do the trick, I run a couple of gags using the *GLO-Loop:* "Watch closely, and I'll give my impression of the famous dancing waters at Disney's Epcot Center. Now, I'll give my impression of Old Faithful, the geyser at Yellowstone National Park." I introduce the trick by saying, "I'd like to demonstrate what I thought was impossible a couple of years ago. What you see in my hand is a solid bracelet. I will attempt to pass it through the string which is inside my little gadget. The bracelet will melt through the string like the passing of a ghost through the walls of an ancient castle. There will be no trace of the passage." After I pass the bracelet through the string I ask, "Now, was that a real miracle? How many people thought that was impossible? How do you think that I accomplished this impossible feat?" After fielding a couple of responses, I recite the poem *It Can't Be Done:*

It Can't Be Done

The ones who miss all of the fun
Are those who say, "It can't be done."
In solemn pride they stand aloof
And greet each venture with reproof.
Had they the power they'd efface
the history of the human race;
We'd have no radio or trolley cars,
No streets lit by electric stars;
No telegraph or telephone,
We'd linger in the age of stone.
The world would sleep
if things were run
By those who say "It can't be done."

Unknown

Color-Changing Scarf

Reasonable men adapt themselves to their environment; unreasonable men try to adapt their environment to themselves, thus all progress is the result of the efforts of the unreasonable men.

—*George Bernard Shaw*

Background

I was looking for a magic trick that would illustrate the concept of change, and found this trick at a magic conference. I've been using this trick in presentations dealing with change.

The Magical Effect

A blue and red scarf becomes yellow and green as it passes between your hands (Fig. 47-1).

Applying the Magic to Presenting and Training

You can use this trick to open discussions about change. You can also use it to discuss perceptions and perceptiveness. If you perform the trick nonchalantly while speaking some people will not notice the change in color. You can take advantage of this occurrence and begin a discussion about paradigms. You can say that some people suffer from "paradigm paralysis," meaning that they are stuck on a particular paradigm despite its obvious problems.

Materials

- 1 color-changing magic scarf or silk streamer. Either one costs $10–$25 and they are available at most magic shops.

The Trick, Step by Step

Follow the directions that come with the scarf.

Sample Patter

As I deliver the following monologue, I pass a magic scarf between my hands, changing its colors. "We're all prisoners of our experiences. Overcoming conventional wisdom was never easy. For centuries, people believed that Aristotle was right when he contended that the heavier an object was, the faster it would fall to earth. Aristotle was regarded as the greatest thinker of all times, so people thought he could not be wrong. But all it would have taken to test his idea was for one brave person to take two objects, one heavy and one light, and drop them from a great height. No one was brave enough until nearly 2000 years after Aristotle's death. In 1589, Galileo summoned learned professors to the base of the Leaning Tower of Pisa. Then he went to the top and dropped a ten-pound and a one-pound ball. They landed at the same time. But the professors denied what they saw. They continued to say Aristotle was right.

"How could this happen? There are many reasons. People have filters and biases, or they are in what Joel Barker calls 'paradigm paralysis.' Everyone is a prisoner of his or her own experience. The key issue is one's ability to handle change, to be comfortable with change. In today's world, change happens at an unprecedented pace. How many of you noticed a change in the scarf that I have in my hand? Those who did not are like the professors who refused to be convinced by Galileo's demonstration. You didn't see change because you weren't looking for change. Or is it that your eyes saw change but your head didn't want to believe it?"

Figure 47-1

Background

I found this trick at a conference of the International Brotherhood of Magicians. Initially, I wasn't exactly sure how I would use it, but eventually I invented a good approach, using the Seven Magic Principles.

The Magical Effect

A $100 bill is locked inside a plastic case with a padlock. Four volunteers are asked to choose one of five keys and try to open the case. None of them succeed. You take the one remaining key and open the lock.

Applying the Magic to Presenting and Training

This is a great trick to open a seminar on perseverance. Anyone who has juggled a ring full of keys knows that it's always the last key that opens the door. You can also use this trick to address marketing systems. What is the key to attracting customers? What key will unlock the market for you? There are many ways to have fun with this trick. Once I put on an ape costume and challenged everyone to outsmart the ape by picking the right key. It had a hilarious effect, since no one outsmarted the ape!

Materials

- 1 magic lock and keys set. This is the most expensive prop in this book; it costs $25–$50. Several brands are available. Most magic shops carry them. I use *The Wonderlock* by Mick Hanzlik (Fig. 48-1).
- 1 hat

It's the Last Key That Opens the Door

Keep on trying. It's often the last key that opens the door.

—*Unknown*

159

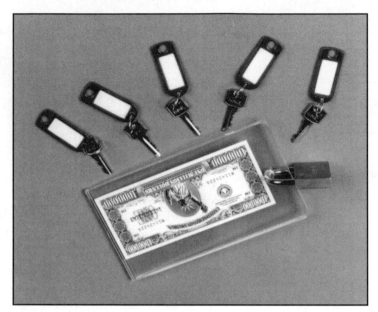

Figure 48-1

The Trick, Step by Step

Step 1:

Demonstrate to the audience that one of the five keys opens the lock. Put all five keys into a hat.

Step 2:

Ask four volunteers each to pick a key from the hat and try to open the lock. Take the fifth key and open the lock (the trick to opening

the lock is explained in the instructions to the magic lock and keys set).

Sample Patter

"I've locked a $100 bill inside this case. There are five keys, one of which opens the lock. If one of you greedy—I mean lucky—people selects the right key and opens the lock, you can have it." I demonstrate that one of the five keys indeed opens the lock, then I re-lock the case. I select four volunteers and let them each choose a key out of a hat. I take the fifth key. Before I let them try out their keys, I offer to exchange mine with theirs. After a volunteer has tried his or her key, I again offer to exchange keys with the remaining volunteers. This makes the audience think that there is one right key.

When I finally open the lock with my key I give a sign of relief and exclaim, "Well, I guess I'll be able to buy food for the kids this week!" I conclude, "It's often the last key that opens the door. We must persevere if we want to succeed."

Background

Duane Laflin of Sterling Company told me how he uses this trick to introduce key concepts to his church youth group. I use it in my seminars on teamwork to draw attention to the word "respect."

The Magical Effect

A plastic holder holds tiles that have letters on them (Fig. 49-1). The letters do not spell a word. The holder is turned away from the audience and the tiles are taken out. The tiles are re-inserted into the holder according to the audience's directions. When the holder is turned toward the audience, the letters spell "respect" (Fig. 49-2).

Applying the Magic to Presenting and Training

You can use this trick to draw attention to any keyword relevant to your presentation. I use it in team-building seminars to focus attention on the word "respect." Sometimes I use it with young people as my friend Duane Laflin has; I used it to begin a discussion about mutual respect with high school and junior high school students.

Materials

- 1 children's spelling-bee set. They cost around $25 and are available at most toy stores.
- A table

Trick #**49**

Magic Keyword Speller

There are three kinds of lies: lies, damned lies and statistics.

—*Unknown*

161

Figure 49-1

Figure 49-2

The Trick, Step by Step

Step 1:

Select tiles so that they spell the word you want, and cut each tile so that it fits in the plastic holder without any part of it protruding. Insert the selected tiles in the holder so that they spell the word you want.

Step 2:

Select another set of tiles that spell the same word. Insert this set of tiles in the holder in random order, putting them *in front of* the first set of tiles. The first set should be hidden behind the second set, and it should appear as if there is only one tile in each slot.

Step 3:

Show the holder to the audience, pointing out that the letters do not spell a word. Turn the holder away from the audience. Pull out the second set of tiles, placing them face down on a table. Mix the tiles on the table.

Step 4:

Pick up a tile and ask the audience in which slot you should put the tile. Put the tile in the slot specified by the audience, *behind the hidden tile*. Repeat with the remaining tiles. Turn the holder around and show it to the audience.

Sample Patter

Showing the spelling-bee set to the audience (Fig. 49-1) I explain that I brought it in to spell out some keywords relevant to the presentation. Before I take out the tiles I like to joke, "Right now the letters don't spell anything. It can't possibly spell 'anything' because 'anything' consists of eight letters and I only have seven letters here!" While I take out the tiles and place them on the table, I ask the audience to think of a word that is foundational to teamwork. I ask them to concentrate on the word silently. Picking up a tile from the table, I ask a person in the audience which slot I should put it in, then put it in the specified slot. I repeat with the remaining tiles. As I turn the plastic holder around, I muse that everyone must have thought of the word "respect" since the letters arranged themselves to spell that word (Fig. 49-2). I conclude, "Respect is indeed the foundation of all team-work. Mutual respect generates trust and trust is the glue that holds a team together. A team cannot remain together without respect."

Background

This trick inspired me to use magic tricks in my presentations. It is the first magic trick I saw integrated with a presentation and it is also the first magic trick I learned. When I saw it I was so impressed I wished, "If only I could do that." Well, guess what? I not only learned this trick but dozens of others, and began using them in my presentations. Once you use this trick in your presentation, you will be hooked on magic, just as I was.

The Magical Effect

A volunteer is given an invisible deck of cards and asked to pick a card, memorize it, flip it over, and put it back in the deck. The invisible deck is tossed to you, which then becomes visible. When you fan out the deck the card selected by the volunteer is face down.

Applying the Magic to Presenting and Training

This trick can be linked to the concept of probability with questions like, "What is the probability that the right card flipped itself over?" It can be used to lead into a discussion about perception and imagination with questions like, "Who can see the invisible deck and who cannot?" It can be used to discuss motivation, dreams, and ambition, with questions like, "Who believed that the invisible deck could become real?"

Invisible Cards

Our wildest dreams sometimes become our greatest successes.

—*Unknown*

Materials

- 1 *Invisible Deck of Cards.* This is available at most magic shops. Haines' House of Cards (2514 Leslie Ave., Norwood, OH 45212, (513) 531-6548) has them at a discount price.

The Trick, Step by Step

Step 1:

Explain to a volunteer that you are going to throw him or her an invisible deck of cards. Make a throwing motion. Ask the volunteer to shuffle the deck. Ask another volunteer to select a card from the deck, memorize it, flip it over, and put it back in the deck.

Step 2:

Palm the *Invisible Deck of Cards* in your hand and ask the first volunteer to toss the invisible deck back to you. When she or he does, make a catching motion and show the *Invisible Deck of Cards* (Fig. 50-1). This makes it appear as if the invisible deck became visible as you caught it.

Step 3:

Ask the second volunteer to tell everyone the identity of the card she or he selected. Show the cards in the *Invisible Deck of Cards* to the audience (follow directions for *Invisible Deck of Cards* for manipulating the selected card).

Sample Patter

I announce to my audience that I have an invisible deck of cards and ask if they can see it. When someone says yes, I look astonished and say, "You must have better eyes than I do!" I toss the invisible deck to a volunteer and ask her or him to shuffle it. Most volunteers will make a shuffling motion immediately, and I say, "Don't you want to take the cards out of the box first?" or "You must be a magician because you can shuffle the cards without taking them out of the box." Some volunteers become stunned and don't know what to do with an invisible deck of cards in an invisible case. I goad them lightheartedly, "Don't make a career out of it, just shuffle the deck."

When the deck is tossed back to me, I congratulate the volunteer with: "Great throw," and leave a moment of silence for the audience to digest the appearance of the visible deck in my hand. Then I ask the volunteer who selected a card from the invisible deck to tell everyone which card was selected. Often the volunteer cannot respond immediately because she or he hadn't actually thought of a card yet. That's okay. I give the person a moment to invent a card's identity. Once the identity of the card is announced, I open the case of *Invisible Deck of Cards* and show the deck to the audience. By this point, of course, the right card has been flipped over (Fig. 50-2).

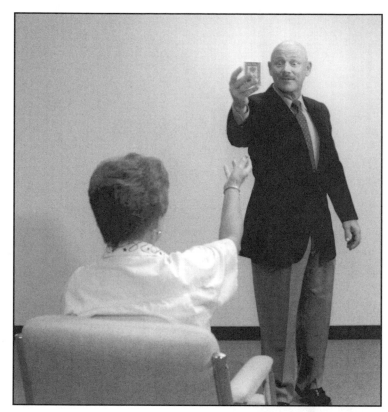

Figure 50-1

Figure 50-2

Background
This is a common magic trick, adapted here for use in presentations. It's easy to learn and use.

The Magical Effect

You open a book on a hot topic and flames come out of it.

Applying the Magic to Presenting and Training

You can use this trick with any topic—just design an appropriate book cover. For example, for my conflict-resolution workshops, I designed a book cover that reads, *"Three Hot Ways to Manage Conflict."* It works equally well to grab attention at the beginning of a presentation or to wrap up a presentation with a visual device.

Materials

- 1 flaming book (available at most magic shops)
- 1 custom cover for the book
- Lighter fluid

Note: It is possible to make a flaming book yourself by attaching a lighter to an aluminum-lined hole in an old book (Fig. 51-2). This is difficult work, however, and often the effect isn't as good as that produced by a store-bought flaming book, so I do not recommend it.

The Trick, Step by Step

Step 1:

Introduce the book, then open it and the flames shoot up.

#51
Trick

A Hot Topic

The mind is like a TV set; when it goes blank, it's a good idea to turn off the sound.
—*Unknown*

169

Figure 51-1

Step 2:

Slam the book shut, smile, and say that the topic must be too hot for the audience.

Sample Patter

I open my conflict-resolution workshop by showing my book to the audience and saying, "I'd like to read from the best-selling book, *Three Hot Ways to Manage Conflict,* by Steve 'Flaming' Buckley. "As I open the book, flames shoot out and I slam it shut. I say, "I think that's a little too hot for this class" (Fig. 51-1).

I close some of my presentations using the flaming book. When the flames shoot out, I slam the book shut and say, "Whoa! Do you know what that was all about? Well, I always wanted to end my presentation in a blaze of fire!"

Figure 51-2

Background

Levitating an object has captured people's wonder and amazement for thousands of years. It should be a part of every magician's—and presenter's—repertoire. Floating a dollar bill is a great way to learn to levitate objects. It takes a bit of practice to perfect, but the effect is worth every minute of preparation.

The Magical Effect

A dollar bill you borrowed from the audience floats between your hands, in mid-air (Fig. 52-1).

Applying the Magic to Presenting and Training

Now that I've mastered the technique, I float a bill every chance I get. My favorite venue, though, is at business dinners and other informal meetings. Once you've captured their attention, people will hang on your every word. I've used the trick occasionally to introduce a workshop on the power of positive thinking— the energy from my positive thinking levitates the dollar bill.

Materials

- Invisible thread (available at most magic shops)

Note: Various gadgets are available at magic shops for levitating bills. They range in price from a few dollars to $40 or $60. My favorite is the new invisible thread created by George Proust in Paris. Find the type that is made to fit over your wrist so that there is minimal setup required. This thread should cost only $2 per loop and is reusable.

Floating Dollar Bill

Poise is the ability to keep talking while the other person pays the check.

—*Unknown*

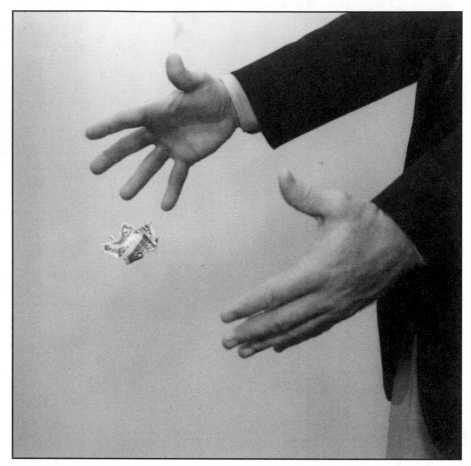

Figure 52-1

The Trick, Step by Step

Step 1:

Borrow a dollar bill from the audience (or live dangerously and borrow a larger denomination bill!).

Step 2:

Begin talking, and float the bill between your hands (follow directions on the package of invisible thread).

Sample Patter

At a seminar on positive thinking, I begin "I'd like to demonstrate what I learned from this course the first time I studied it. May I borrow a dollar bill from someone?" Borrowing the bill makes the audience think that the bill isn't rigged. "What is possible through positive thinking? Can we alter our own behaviors through positive thinking? Can we alter other people's behaviors through positive thinking? Can we even alter the behavior of inanimate objects through positive thinking?" As I speak, I float the bill between my hands rather casually. After about a minute of talking while floating the bill, I return the bill to the audience and launch into my seminar and do not give the audience too much time to analyze the trick.

Background

When you do this trick your audience will think you're the next David Copperfield. **David Copperfield?** Yes, he performed this trick on television. It's a popular trick among professional magicians, even though it's very simple to perform. I adapted it into a "visual check" routine to start presentations. You'll see why it's a popular trick when you see the eyes of your audience light up.

The Magical Effect

You hold a rose stem (with no flower) and set an end on fire (Fig. 53-1). When you extinguish the flame (Fig. 53-2), a rose appears on the stem (Fig. 53-3).

Applying the Magic to Presenting and Training

I use the trick as a "visual check" at the start of a presentation—it's a check to make sure everyone can see me well. If the audience cannot see the rose they won't be able to see my charts and slides, so I have them reposition themselves. Fire is a great attention-grabber. I performed this trick to begin a talk on teamwork for 400 high school students. When I lit the stem on fire 400 pairs of unblinking eyes immediately focused on me, anxious to see what would happen next!

Materials

- 1 *Phantom Rose* by Jair Bonair. This is inexpensive and available at most magic shops.

Fire to Rose

Some succeed because they are destined to. Most succeed because they are determined to.

—*Unknown*

Figure 53-1

Figure 53-2

Note: There are other brands of "Fire to Rose" magic kits available, but I cannot recommend them. Jair Bonair was the first to design and market a "Fire to Rose" magic kit. His product is of high quality and has a proven history.

- Lighter fluid
- Lighter

The Trick, Step by Step

Follow directions on the "Fire to Rose" magic kit.

Sample Patter

I stand in front of my audience, light the stem on fire, and say, "This is a visual check to make sure everyone can see what's happening up here. If you can't see me well, please move closer. Now, watch closely." I extinguish the flame and a rose appears. Then I do an "audio check" to make sure that everyone can hear me well.

Figure 53-3

Closing Comments

Hopefully, in the course of perusing this book, you discovered several tricks that complement your presentation and personality.

I'd like to close with a few words about your "stage presence." There are specific techniques for structuring a presentation. There are discrete rules you should follow when presenting. But techniques and rules are not enough. If you rely on them alone, you will fall short of your goal—to make a profound impression on your audience. Your presentation will miss that "je ne sais quoi."

Without that "little something" the audience won't buy what you're selling. Just what is that little something? Often it's humor. More generally, it is personality. The chemistry between the presenter's personality and those of the people in the audience is what generates a sense of amusement, like (or dislike), trust, and respect. Most people know how to project personality, although most of the time it is done unconsciously. A presenter must become aware of his or her personality and learn to project it effectively.

What is your personality? How can you use it effectively? Unfortunately, the answers fall in the realm of art, not science. No recipes or rules are available. But we can approach this experientially, by observing and experimenting with intuition and creativity. Let's look at some famous presenters and their personalities.

Actors	Comedians	Magicians	Business Presenters	Ministers
Jack Nicholson	David Letterman	David Copperfield	Steven Covey	Billy Graham
Glenn Close	Lily Tomlin	Siegfried & Roy	Ken Blanchard	Oral Roberts
	Jerry Lewis			

Each of these people has a unique personality that is easily recognized. When they are in front of an audience, that "little something" in their personalities initially draws the audience's attention. They have stage presence. Their stage presence prepares the audience to listen attentively. Even an actor who plays different characters has something very special in his or her personality that is essential; the actor's essence is *present* in all the characters he or she plays. Every presenter should strive to understand how to improve this stage presence—how to enhance that "little something" in his or her personality—and consider how that may draw the audience's attention.

You can develop your stage presence by focusing on what I call **ESP—E**nergy, **S**tyle, and **P**ersonality. What drives your stage presence (the heart of it) will be **energy.** Energy is necessary to project your message to the audience. Don't force it; let your natural enthusiasm radiate. Energy is communicated through a friendly posture and lively body movements. Confidence is appealing to the audience. Confidence comes from practice, practice, and more practice.

The second component of ESP is **style.** Your style must fit you well. It must be believable. Ask yourself what it is about your background that would interest the audience. This can range from education to job, family, or traveling experience—anything that makes you a little differ-

ent. How you perform the magic tricks in this book will shape your style. Other key factors are dress, voice, facial expressions, and personal features.

The third component of ESP is **personality.** Take a good look at yourself and decide what qualities you have that make you different from other people. If you can't find any, you're not looking hard enough. We all have unique talents and experiences. What is unique about you that gives you strength or insight? Are you knowledgeable in a unique topic? Do you have a unique talent? Audiences can usually see right through fakes, so don't try to be someone you're not.

ESP is all about charisma. When you have perfected your energy level, style, and personality, you will have charisma—and you'll be a better presenter![1]

I began writing this book to help other corporate trainers. To my surprise, my manuscript proved to be useful for coaches, teachers, salespersons, and businesspeople. Magic can enhance any message a person wants to communicate. Don't worry about your lack of magic experience. I am a mere neophyte magician myself, but as they say, "amateurs built the ark; professionals built the Titanic." If you have any problems understanding a trick, feel free to e-mail me at ER1495@AOL.COM. I will help you.

Enjoy!

Ed Rose

[1]For more information on *Showmanship for Presenters* read Dave Arch's book by that title, published by Creative Training Techniques Press.

Bibliography and Resources

Publications

Harry Allen, *Sleight of One Liners,* Daytona Beach, FL: Harry Allen, 1991.

Friedhoffer, *Magic Tricks, Scientific Facts,* NY, NY: Franklin Watts, 1990.

K. Fulves, *More Self-Working Card Tricks,* NY, NY: Dover Publications, 1984.

F. Garcia and G. Schindler, *Magic with Cards,* NY, NY: Barnes & Noble Books.

GENII: The International Conjurors Magazine, P.O. Box 36068, Los Angeles, CA 90036.

W. G. Gibson, *Professional Magic for Amateurs,* NY, NY: Dover Publications, 1974.

H. Hay, *Learn Magic,* NY, NY: Dover Publications, 1975.

B. Herz with P. Harris, *Secrets of the Astonishing Executive,* NY, NY: Avon Books, 1991.

J. Hugard and Braue, *The Royal Road to Card Magic,* London: Faber & Faber, 1975.

Magic Magazine, Stan Allen and Associates, 7380 S. Eastern Ave., Suite 124-179, Las Vegas, NV 89123.

M-U-M, The Society of American Magicians' Monthly Magazine, P.O. Box 338, 26855 Sanders Meadow Rd., Idyllwild, CA 92549.

D. Roper, *The Comedy Magic Textbook,* Norcross, GA: David Ginn, Publisher, 1991.

Magic Societies

The Society of American Magicians
Box 510260
St Louis, MO 63151
(314) 846-5659

International Brotherhood of Magicians
Box 192090
St Louis, MO
(314) 351-7677

International Magicians Society
Tony Hassin, President
NY, NY
(516) 333-6130

Magic Shops

Haines' House of Cards
2514 Leslie Ave.
Norwood, OH 45212
(513) 531-6548

Hank Lee's Magic Factory
P.O. Box 789
Medford, MA 02155
(617) 482-8749

Magic Land
Magic tricks, gag gifts, jokes, costumes,
and makeup.
Howard Hale
Dallas, TX
(215) 350-0966

Michael Ammar Magic
5107 Evergreen Ct.
Austin, TX 78731-5420
(512) 454-7311

Laflin's Magic
Duane and Mary Laflin
Sterling, CO
(303) 522-2589

Mecca Magic, Inc.
Bloomfield, NY
(201) 429-7597

Dan Garrett
4929 Salem Road
Lithonia, GA 30038

Seatle Magic Sentre
Micky Hades
89 S. Washington St.
Seattle, WA 91804
(206) 624-4287

Meir Yedid
Rego Park, NY
(718) 592-6082

Collector's Workshop Misty Morn Farm
Route 1, Box 113A
Middleburg, VA 22117

Empire Magic
Bill and Helen Gormont
99 Stratford Ln.
Rochester, NY 14612
(716) 227-9760

Callin Novelties House of Magic
Conrad J. Weber
412 S.W. 4th Ave.
Portland, OR 97204
(503) 223-4821

Daytona Magic
Harry Allen
136 South Beach St.
Daytona Beach, FL 32114
(904) 254-6767

Stevens Magic Emporium
2520 E. Douglas
Wichita, KS 67214
(316) 683-9582

Rabbit in the Hat Ranch
World's largest mail order magic house.
1017 Crystal Circle
Casselberry, FL 32707-4536
(407) 695-3630

The Joke Shop
265 W. Main St.
Waukesha, WI 53186
(414) 544-5687

Browser's Den of Magic
875 Eglinton Ave., W. - #13
Toronto, ON M6C 3Zg, Canada
(416) 783-7022

Zauberservice
Vestastrasse 8, D-81249
Munchen, Germany
01 1 89 8641374

Arjan's Show-Biz Centre
P.O. Box 368
2920 AJ Krimpen A/D
Yssel, Holland
+31 180 510011

Tokyo Magic Company, Ltd.
2-2-10 Kiba, Kotoku
Tokyo, Japan
03 3630 5074

Egelo
Tordenskiolds gt 12, 0160
Oslo 1, Norway
+22208085

Dick Marvel Magic Studio
Apartado 713
4501 Espinho Codex, Portugal
351-2-723345

El Duco's Magic
Box 31052
200 49 Malmo, Sweden
46 40 21 45 92

Weller Magic
101 13 W. Willowcreek Cir.
Sun City, AZ 85373-1130
(602) 977-9711

Sterling Magic Manufacturing
P.O. Box 228
110 Denver St.
Sterling, CO 80751
(303) 522-2589

Hollywood Magic
298-D East 17th St.
Costa Mesa, CA 92627
(714) 646-4374

Winkler's Warehouse of Wonders
24 Doyle Rd.
Oakdale, CT 06370-1052
(203) 859-3474

Samuel Patrick Smith
P.O. Box 769
Tavares, FL 32778
(904) 357-2665

Eddie's Trick & Novelty Shop, Inc.
262 Rio Circle
Decatur, GA 30030
(404) 377-0003

Chuck's House of Magic
18301 Dixie Highway
Homewood, IL 60430
(708) 798-2111

Stoner's Funstores
5511B Coldwater Rd.
Fort Wayne, IN 46814
(219) 484-9408

Kogel's Magic
6751 Colbert St.
New Orleans, LA 70124-2240
(504) 482-5153

The Electronic Magic Store - Library
Services, Inc.
1498-M Reisterstown Road, #337
Baltimore, MD 21208
(410) 358-8889

Crown Magic & Fun Shop
4202 E. 10 Mile Road
Warrne, MI 48091-1577
(810) 755-9181

Twin Cities Magic & Costume Co.
241 W. 7th St.
St. Paul, MN 55102
(612) 227-7888

Mr. E's Magic & Novelties
314-A E. Pershing St.
Springfield, MO 65806
(417) 862-1968

Don's Magic & Fun Shop
1414-E S. College Rd., Wilmington, NC
28403, (910) 792-0511

Underground Novelties
2324 N. 48th St.
Lincoln, NE 68504-3625
(402) 430-0445

Callin Novelties
412 SW 4th Ave.
Portland, OR 97204-2202
(503) 223-4821

Sasco, Inc.
11609 Proctor Rd.
Philadelphia, PA 19116-2911
(215) 364-7717

The Magic Shop
3600 Fredricksburg Rd., #1270
San Antonio, TX 78201
(210) 699-6033

Up Your Sleeve Discount Magic
P.O. Box 610
Friendswood, TX 77549-0610
(713) 996-5232

World of Magic
P.O. Box 584
Green River, UT 84525-0584
(800) 771-7012

Magic Industries, Inc.
3309 Broad Rock Blvd.
Richmond, VA 23224
(804) 230-1500

Market Magic Shop
1501 Pike Place, #427
Seattle, WA 98101-1542
(206) 624-4271

Robert Swadling, Creators &
Manufacturers of Quality Magic
13 Roman Way
Wantge, Oxon, 0X129YF, England

Las Vegas Magic Shop - Hacienda Hotel
3950 Las Vegas Blvd. S.W.
Las Vegas, NV 89119
(702) 739-1920

The Magic Shop on the Strip -
Riviera Hotel & Casino
2901 Las Vegas Blvd. S.W.
Las Vegas, NV 89109
(702) 733-1965

Mecca Magic, Inc.
49 Dodd St.
Bloomfield, NJ 07003
(201) 429-7597

Wireless Wizardry
4300 Walter Ave.
Parona, OH 44134
(216) 351-4456

About the Author

Ed Rose is the training manager at Harris Semiconductor in Palm Bay, Florida. He has worked in high-technology industries for 32 years with the majority of his experience in manufacturing. Ed has written and produced an extensive training curriculum for team development, and conducts workshops on teamwork and effective team behaviors at local colleges and high schools. He has published several papers on the subject of self-directed work teams in technical journals and magazines, including team-building exercises with McGraw-Hill and Human Resources Development Press. He has served as a quality examiner for the State of Florida and is sought after as a speaker on self-directed work teams and team building.

Since incorporating magic into his presentations and workshops, Ed has been a frequent presenter at national conferences for the Association of Quality and Productivity, the American Society for Training & Development, and the International Conference on Work Teams sponsored by the University of North Texas. He is a member of the International Brotherhood of Magicians and the International Magicians Society. Ed is also President of TLC Consulting, specializing in team building with experiential learning initiatives. Ed's team background is extensive. He has played a variety of team sports, including playing on and coaching more than ten national championship slow-pitch softball teams.

Ed has been successful in using basic magic tricks in unique ways to enhance his presentations, workshops, and team-building sessions around the United States and in Europe. He is not a professional magician, but rather a professional trainer, who views magic as a tool for his work. He believes magic is an excellent way to break old paradigms.

Team Building with Magic and Experiential Learning Initiatives

TLC Consulting - **Trust Leadership Competency** - *"Education will never be as expensive as ignorance."*

Ed Rose, President
5400 Sandlake Dr.
Melbourne, FL 32934
(407) 254-1495